"Daniel Montgomery and Mike Cosper are wise guides for the journey. In *Faithmapping*, they set out a pattern for personal discipleship and the life of the faithful Christian in the local church. I welcome this book."

R. Albert Mohler Jr., President, The Southern Baptist Theological Seminary

"These days, it seems like 'gospel-centered' books are a dime a dozen. Yet *Faithmapping* isn't anything if it's not unique. The missional focus of this contribution to the gospel-centered movement is a breath of fresh air. Well done."

Ed Stetzer, President, LifeWay Research; author, *Subversive Kingdom*

"After knowing Daniel and Mike for years, I can affirm that these men live the words of this book. I highly recommend it for those who are new to Christianity or mature in their faith. The title says it all! It is a trusted navigator for those who desire for Christ to be all."

Darrin Patrick, Lead Pastor, The Journey, St. Louis, Missouri

"*Faithmapping* is excellent. When I wasn't reading it, I was thinking about it, and when I was reading it, I didn't want to put it down. It is theologically profound and yet very easy to read."

Jessica Thompson, coauthor, *Give them Grace*

"Daniel Montgomery and Mike Cosper are human torches, afire with the gospel and igniting the dry kindling all around them. This book, full of gospel beauty and Bible wisdom, can light up the path in front of you, as you walk the path God is stretching out before your feet. Read it, and feel the fire."

Russell D. Moore, Dean, The Southern Baptist Theological Seminary; author, *Tempted and Tried*

FAITHMAPPING

FAITHMAPPING

A Gospel Atlas for Your Spiritual Journey

Daniel Montgomery
and
Mike Cosper

CROSSWAY

WHEATON, ILLINOIS

Library of Congress Cataloging-in-Publication Data

Montgomery, Daniel, 1974–
Faithmapping : a Gospel atlas for your spiritual journey / Daniel Montgomery and Mike Cosper.
   p. cm.
   Includes bibliographical references and index.
   ISBN 978-1-4335-3253-5 (tp)
   1. Christianity—Essence, genius, nature. 2. Christianity—21st century. I. Cosper, Mike, 1980-   II. Title.
BT60.M65   2013
248—dc23   2012024795

Crossway is a publishing ministry of Good News Publishers.

VP		23	22	21	20	19	18	17	16	15	14	13
15	14	13	12	11	10	9	8	7	6	5	4	3	2	1

To our wives,
Sarah and Mandy,
who've faithfully mapped out the connections between
the gospel, the church, and our homes.
This book would have not been possible without you.

Contents

Introduction

If you don't know where you are going,
you might wind up someplace else.

YOGI BERRA

Once upon a time, there were maps. Not Google Maps, not Garmin GPS maps, not MapQuest or Orbitz, but paper maps, printed maps, hand-drawn maps. If you needed directions, you wouldn't pull out a wireless device and punch in an address. You certainly wouldn't speak to it directly. Instead, a friendly stranger or an informed friend might pull out a pen and a napkin and sketch directions. Road trips involved stacks of maps. Big, colorful spreads that tumbled out of glove compartments, marked with state lines and interstate highways, lakes and national parks, showed you not only your destination, but all that was around you, all that you passed on the journey, vast expanses you couldn't possibly visit or explore.

In days even further past, every map was a treasure map. Maps were rare and precious things, and they revealed destinations whose names carried hopes and dreams—places that were supposedly lands of milk and honey, where gold littered streams. These lands were lush and fertile and ready for the industrious explorer, conqueror, or homesteader to claim for his own. Promised lands. New worlds. Mysterious horizons where the seas simply faded into nothing.

When you pull up a route on your phone or GPS device, you're given tailor-made information. Your location and destination are calculated somewhere in cyberspace, and your screen fills up with information that's just for you—where you are, where you're going, and turn-by-turn directions to get you there.

Maps, on the other hand, aren't about you. They're about a place, and they serve as an invitation and a guide. They show how the landscape is pieced together and where the pitfalls are along the way. They show you relationships—how the land and sea interact, how the mountains spill out into plains, how a river carves through a valley. How Broadway slashes across Manhattan from the Lower East Side to the Upper West, or how Little Havana sits in the heart of Miami, along Calle Ocho from 12th to 27th. Whatever your origin and destination may be, it is plotted against the sprawling backdrop of the cities, states, and continents on your map—expanses far beyond your own journey that nonetheless give you a sense of place.

If one day you found yourself beamed, Star Trek–style, from the comforts of your living room into the middle of an unfamiliar wilderness without a map, you would be, in the truest sense of the word, "lost." While the position of the sun might indicate where north, south, east, and west are, you would not know what lies in any of those directions.

Now imagine that a guide appears. He promises that food and shelter lie to the east. Just as you're about to follow him, another guide appears. "No, no! It's to the west!" he says.

They begin bickering about which journey is the best journey, and the tension begins to boil. Suddenly a third, then a fourth, then a fifth guide emerges. Each has a glimmering smile and loud promises to make about how his way is the right way. What would you do in this seemingly hopeless and confusing scenario?

This isn't far from the dilemma of ordinary Christians.

The gospel transfers us from the familiar territory of self-centered living into a glorious wilderness, a beautiful and strange place where we're invited to explore the wonders of who God is and what he's done. It's exciting and frightening, and when we set out on our journey, we quickly find ourselves bombarded by a host of loud, demanding voices telling us how the journey is meant to unfold, where we're meant to go, and how we're meant to get there. There's often no coherence among the voices. Some tell us that the journey is a way of discipleship, others say that it's a way of service or worship. Each voice describes its way as central and primary, shouting over the others and echoing in the hills, a harsh cacophony of chaos.

The Christian stands in the midst of these competing voices, searching for a reliable guide and a way forward. The noise leads to confusion, and in the midst of confusion, it's often the loudest voice that wins. We buy into the hype and follow along, watching as competing voices bicker and divide. Before long, there's a sense of dissatisfaction, a fear that perhaps we're on the wrong path, and soon we turn off the path to follow another voice, repeating the same pattern.

It's a predictable cycle, a song in four movements that plays out again and again in the life of the church. It's a cycle of:

Confusion
Hype
Division
Instability

Confusion

The cycle begins with confusion. Ever since the Tower of Babel, human beings have faced serious communication obstacles. Language is constantly evolving, and the language one generation uses to give clarity and definition to the gospel is likely to need fresh revision and nuance in just a few years. In addition, there's a temptation to take what the Scriptures tell us about the gospel and either complicate it beyond comprehensibility (with academic jargon and insider language), or hack it to pieces in the name of "simplification." Simplifying can mean watering down the bold claims of the gospel, or it can mean emphasizing one aspect of the gospel to the exclusion of the others. Both errors distort the glorious message with which the church has been entrusted.

The great need in the church is for simple (but not simplistic) definition. By "definition," we mean both an explanation that makes something comprehensible and the quality of being sharp and clear. We need to clarify what we mean when we use basic terms like *gospel*, *church*, and *mission* in order to bring clarity to the mission to which God is calling his church.

God is not a God of confusion. At the Tower of Babel, sin brought a new and powerful confusion, disorder, and division to the world, but at Pentecost, the gospel was put on display as God's means for reuniting the world. Language that can divide, can also, by God's grace, unite people under the banner of King Jesus. We believe that the Scriptures are both clear and sufficient for informing us about the gospel, church, and mission. They give us a clear destination toward which we can lock arms and journey together.

Hype

Confusion gives birth to the second stage of the cycle. The easy way to cut through the noise of confusion is with hype: loud, exaggerated spiritual promises. Hype is "excessive publicity and the ensuing commotion" or "exaggerated or extravagant claims made especially in advertising or promotional material."

Hype is a symptom of a major cultural disease. We are the target of constant marketing that promises happiness if we buy this or that; we're drawn to glittering images of the "good life." Hype is at the heart of selling, and it's so pervasive that it transforms the way we talk about everything from worship to fast food. Everything we do is "awesome," "spectacular," or "epic." We're perpetually one-upping ourselves with new products, new schemes, and, in the church, new religious methodology.

Confusion sends Christians on a search for clarity, but they find themselves settling for hype instead. The loudest voices, the best-marketed voices, or (in many cases) the timely reactionary voices substitute for clarity. The timely reactionary voice is the person whose approach is a response to the overemphasis of the previous generation. As one generation or one tribe emphasizes one aspect of the gospel, that aspect becomes central. Then, a few years (or months) later, another tribe reacts against that overemphasis, and a new fad is born with a new overemphasis. So the church is in a constant state of whiplash, being told in one season that the gospel is all about missions and evangelism, in another that it's all about discipleship, in yet another that it's all about worship, and so on.

Hype is supported by a commercial machine, marketing it and inducing the crowd into a fad-chasing frenzy. We're bombarded with the new book, the new conference, the new celebrity pastor offering to be our guide to spiritual bliss. What's sold, though, is often a gospel reduced to simplistic principles or patterns of behavior.

It's a horrible disservice to what Karl Barth called the "strange new world of the Bible," a story spanning generations, involving miracles and mystics, visionaries, kings, and killers—sometimes all in the same character.[1] This glorious story is wild and untamed, something that we'll never encapsulate in the sound bites and catchphrases of marketed hype. Our search for clarity needs to be willing to accept the depth, width, and complexity of a whole gospel.

Instead, pastors get drunk on fads, driving their churches while under the influence, leaving congregations dizzy as they careen from fad to fad. Over the years, everyone gets a spiritual hangover, unable to get excited about the new thing, wondering why it feels like something is missing.

Division

The inevitable result is division. Fads lead to factions; people committed to one fad usually position themselves against another fad, rallying around their fad and declaring war on the opposition. Churches divide and denominations and movements form when one good thing becomes everything.

Instead of settling for factions, we need to strive for unity. We need to make the connections between gospel, church, and world for the sake of the unity that Jesus prayed for (John 17).

Instability

All of this confusion, hype, and division leads to the constant state of instability we see in North American churches. It's evident in the revolving doors in our churches, where members, leaders, and pastors whirl in and out the door in regular, rhythmic rotations.

Desperate for guidance, Christians drift from church to church and craze to craze, forfeiting a patient, biblical, holistic approach in exchange for guidance from gurus, consultants, armchair theologians, bloggers, ivory tower academics, and church conference craziness. This drifting is not unlike the "church camp yo-yo." Every summer, the emotional roller coaster of church camp leads kids to rededicate their lives to Jesus, convinced that this time, with new insights, with this new powerful experience under their belts, they've finally "got it." It's a predictable emotional cycle, with kids getting baptized and rebaptized, and rebaptized again because now, at last, they've found the holy grail. Though the cycle may be a bit more subtle, adults do the same thing.

Including pastors.

What we're actually hungry for is stability. We want a faith that has a sense of rootedness, that isn't tossed about by marketing fads and celebrity pastors. We want something with history and depth, a reliable guide for our spiritual journey. We need a map that shows us the way through the wilderness, one with the breadth and perspective that shows us where we are, where we're going, and what's around us, with an invitation to explore and discover the wonders of God's kingdom with God's church in God's world.

The prophet Jeremiah described such a way when he said:

> Thus says the LORD:
> "Stand by the roads, and look,
>   and ask for the ancient paths,
> where the good way is; and walk in it,
>   and find rest for your souls." (Jer. 6:16)

The alternative to the never-ending carousel of confusion and fads is an ancient path, an old way that saints have followed for a long, long time. It's a way opened by the good news of the gospel.

Faithmapping is our attempt to identify that ancient path through the wilderness by mapping out our mission. We want to illustrate the connections between what God has done in the gospel, who we are as the church, and how we are to live in the world. It's an exploration of a whole gospel for a whole church for the sake of the whole world.

It's not something that we invented or discovered, but something that wise voices in the church have clearly and patiently articulated again and again. And it's a lesson that we discovered the hard way. We, like so many, have wrestled with the seduction of ministry fads and found ourselves on the search for a "holy grail" of ministry philosophy, jumping from trend to trend, looking desperately for a way that would make sense of ministry and give us a clear sense of focus.

In many ways, I (Daniel) discerned my sense of calling while planting Sojourn. I had come to seminary with a vague sense of a calling, but without a great desire to be a pastor. I was attracted to church planting (through the mentoring of Ed Stetzer) in part because I had strong entrepreneurial ambitions.

When Sojourn launched, I was a twenty-five-year-old patriarch. The church's average age was twenty (with many in their teens) and the fact that I was married, educated, and had my own apartment set me apart from the congregation of young, wandering Christians. I spent the early years at Sojourn wandering the multifaceted maze of evangelical Christianity, trying to figure out who I was, what a pastor was, and what it meant to be the church.

Before long, I was overwhelmed, juggling the roles of church planter, leader, preacher, pastor, husband, father, and friend. I wanted to "get it right," but couldn't seem to make the roles fit together in a way that had integrity or coherence. I remember breaking down while praying with some of Sojourn's elders, broken over my failure as a father. The absence of my own father loomed over me and filled me with fear; I had to get it together. I had to get it right so I would leave a better legacy.

Church life was overwhelming, too. I was trying to hold together all the bits and pieces that I was learning about what it meant to be the church, bouncing from one big thing to the next. Preaching, church planting, elders, polity, spiritual formation, mercy, evangelism, leadership development: all of these issues emerged in the life of the church and I piled them together like the Clampett's truck, a big, cumbersome, rattling beast journeying down the road. Each issue seemed urgent and all-inclusive, and each book argued that its pet topic was the most important thing in the life of a healthy church.

I grew more confused by all the methodological fads, theological fragments, and divisive factions within the church. There was no end to the hype over the next big thing. I would buy all the books and go to the conferences (or even host conferences). We were always searching for the right formula for doing church, and every voice promised that it had the most promising formula, whether it was getting church government right or practicing the right spiritual discipline.

Frustration and confusion reached a boiling point. The church was growing, gathering about three hundred people on Sundays. We had become self-supporting with multiple staff (something we were told would never happen), and were planting new churches; but in spite of it all, I was ready to step down. It seemed like I had taken the church as far as I could. I thought I might pass Sojourn on to another leader, then move on to plant another church. I often considered changing to another career altogether. It was no longer a mystery to me why so many pastors have short tenures in churches and ministry.

My angst climaxed one night in a community group meeting. About fifteen people gathered in an apartment, and I gave out the assignment to break up into pairs and meditate on Psalm 51. We were to take some time to confess our sins, genuinely and specifically. For me, something unexpected happened. As I was confessing my sins, I was overwhelmed by my weakness and insufficiency. Then, out of nowhere, I was equally overwhelmed by the beauty and sufficiency of my Savior, Jesus Christ. I can't explain how it happened—this certainly wasn't new information, but it was information that I heard and received newly. It's what Jared Wilson calls "gospel wakefulness," a deeper and more powerful personal conviction of the wonder of the gospel.[2]

I felt a new conviction of the power of the cross. With a renewed depth, I saw that Jesus was enough, and that his work was actually able to cover and take away my sins.

Out of that new conviction came new connections. In Psalm 51, David makes a connection between forgiveness and missions—he wants to tell the world what God has accomplished. For me, personal renewal and personal evangelism had always seemed categorically disconnected, two priorities that would push against one another and battle for time and resources. Suddenly I saw how the gospel held them together, how they fueled one another. The gospel that saves us motivates us to live on mission.

Eventually, more and more connections came. I saw that the gospel changes everything, and that it's the central fact of the Christian life, holding all of the diffuse and seemingly distinct priorities together in a beautiful and coherent whole. It's all about Jesus, about what he's done and how he's restored us to life with God—life the way it's meant to be lived.

What emerged was a new vision for pastoring the local church. I was filled with a hunger to help the people of Sojourn make connections between God's gospel and the rest of their lives, their mission, their place in his kingdom. It all held together in Jesus, and I wanted to take a hammer to the way we did church in order to put the gospel at the center of everything.

In a similar way, God had been working on Mike's vision for ministry, and together we began to look at every aspect of the life of Sojourn, asking ourselves, "How does the gospel inform and transform everything we do? How does that message tie together all of our ministry and all of our community?"

We have struggled with those questions for many years now, continuing, even as we write this book, to refine and deepen the way we see its implications. Mike Bullmore casts a vision for this way of doing church when he says:

> A local church is healthy to the degree that: 1) its pastors-teachers are able to accurately, effectively and broadly bring the gospel to bear spe-

cifically into the real lives of the people; and 2) its people have a deep personal understanding of and a deep personal appreciation for the gospel so as to be able to live in the good of the gospel daily.[3]

Faithmapping is our attempt to lay out the lessons we've learned as we've tried, failed, and fallen in love with the gospel. In particular, it's an attempt to show the wonderful landscape of the gospel (part 1), the church (part 2), and our mission (part 3). It is nothing new, but something that's not often said. There is no holy grail. There is no perfect methodology. There is no perfect way to do and be the church. There is only a perfect and sufficient gospel that informs and transforms every aspect of our lives, and fills every step of the journey with surprising joy, life, and hope.

The Whole Gospel—One Gospel, Three Aspects

The North American church is currently in the midst of a bit of a gospel craze. There are countless books and conferences and conference workshops that include "gospel" somewhere in the title, and the phrase "gospel-centered" has become a modifier for almost anything in church (gospel-centered music, gospel-centered preaching, gospel-centered coloring books, gospel-centered greeting ministry, etc.).

In principle, a gospel obsession is the best kind of craze, but it comes with certain risks. When you press into what people mean when they say "gospel," they can mean anything from religious moralism to political activism to a spiritual get-out-of-jail-free card. There is much agreement on the need for a gospel, and much confusion as to what that gospel is.

Even among faithful, Bible-believing Christians, "gospel" can be a confusing and conflict-inducing term. Some define it strictly in terms of the work of Jesus on the cross, and others talk about God's kingdom and rule. Still others talk about grace—radical, scandalous, free grace—as the essential message of the gospel.

Rather than somehow pitting the cross of Christ against the kingdom of Christ or the grace of God for centrality in the message of the gospel, we want to hold them all together, arguing that they are all ways of talking about the gospel, and that they lead to one another if you understand them properly.

This approach to the gospel (sometimes referred to as triperspectivalism) has been argued wonderfully by theologian John Frame and pastor Timothy Keller.[4]

Keller argues that there are three frameworks, or lenses, or aspects to the gospel—three ways to understand the gospel that are equally true and central for the Christian on his or her journey:

1. The gospel of Christ is the historical truth of Jesus, who lived, died, and was resurrected, paying for our sins with his life.
2. The gospel of sonship is about God's radical, transforming, adopting grace. It's about God's accepting us because he accepts Jesus and not because of anything we've done.
3. The gospel of the kingdom is about God's kingdom coming to earth through Jesus and through the church. It's about the renewal of creation, the new-making of all things, a cosmic redemption project that has been inaugurated by Jesus.

The tendency, Keller argues, is to latch onto one or another of these aspects to the exclusion of the others. If we tend to see legalistic moralism as the problem, Keller says, we'll gravitate toward the gospel of sonship "with more emphasis on . . . emotional freedom."[5] Likewise, if we tend to think that Christians are too relativistic and don't respect God's law, we'll gravitate toward the gospel of Christ, which puts our sins on display in the crucified body of Jesus.

It's the pitfall of overreaction. We overreact to sinfulness and become Pharisees. We overreact to Pharisees and become hellions. One generation preaches only the cross, and the next "discovers" the kingdom of God, tossing the cross out of the conversation. As Scotty Smith, founding pastor of Christ Community Church in Franklin, Tennessee, says, "Overreaction usually leads to overcorrection—a lesson I am continually learning, especially in spiritual matters.[6]

It's because of this cycle of overreaction and overcorrection that we need a broader, multifaceted perspective on the gospel. Such a perspective "resolves many traditional arguments; it encourages balance in preaching; and it encourages church unity."[7]

Our tendency toward pharisaism can be tempered by looking at God's scandalous grace. Our tendency toward individualism can be corrected by looking at God's kingdom, a transgenerational, global movement of new-making. And our tendency toward triumphalism and pride can be confronted with the crucified Savior, whose wounds are an eternal reminder of our sin and need.

This isn't to say that these aspects are defined in exclusion of each other. In fact, as Keller says, "if you go deep enough into any one perspective, you will find the other two."[8] The kingdom of God isn't possible without the cross. Likewise, the cross is best understood in the context of a war of kingdoms (of which it is the decisive victory).

Our goal in chapters 1–4 will be to put each of the aspects on display. Chapter 1 ("The Gospel of the Kingdom") argues that the gospel is a kingdom announcement, and it explores what the kingdom of God is, as well as the kingdoms that compete for our hearts and minds. Chapter 2 ("The Gospel of the Cross") argues that the gospel is the story of Jesus's life, death, and resurrection—all that he did to pay the penalty for our sins. Chapter 3 ("The Gospel of Grace") argues that the gospel is a gift of grace, something that God accomplishes for us entirely by his own strength and power, not because we earned or deserved anything. Chapter 4 ("Why We Need a Whole Gospel") talks more about the gospel in three aspects and deals with some of the dangers of a divorced or separated gospel.

It's no mistake that our aspects have a lot in common with Keller's perspectives. John Ortberg, in the introduction to his work on spiritual formation, said that he was so influenced by Dallas Willard that he was tempted to call his book *Dallas for Dummies*.[9] We are deeply indebted to Dr. Keller's preaching and teaching on this topic, and are likewise tempted to title the book, *Keller for Dummies*.

The Whole Church

Much lip service is paid to gospel-centered ministry, but confusion abounds as to what exactly that means and looks like. Too often, we're given the impression that life after faith in Christ is met with a burdensome list of things to do, but there appears to be none of that burden in the book of Acts. Instead, people who've been hit with the gospel respond naturally with radically changed lives and hearts. The church and the ministries of the church are gospel centered when they flow from hearts that are afire with wonder at the glory and grace of God, revealed in the person of Jesus.

After exploring and sketching out a map of the gospel, we'll begin to shade in the way it transforms us. The gospel doesn't give us a new set of obligations and duties—it gives us a new identity. What we do flows from who we are—a gospel-formed people who are radically transformed.

Part 2 ("The Whole Church") unpacks the movement of transformation: how the gospel changes us from the inside out, and how that differs from the way the world understands religion and change. Chapters 5–9 are each focused on a gospel-formed aspect to our new identity:

Chapter 5: Worshipers
Chapter 6: Family
Chapter 7: Servants
Chapter 8: Disciples
Chapter 9: Witnesses

The Whole World

In chapter 10, we will seek to make the connection between these gospel-formed identities and the world we inhabit. We live them out as the church before the eyes of the world, a testimony to God's relentless and magnificent work of grace. We're not made into a church and left in a holy huddle. We're invited to journey onward and outward into the world, participating in God's new-making of creation, living out those identities and bearing witness to God's gospel to the whole world, including our:

Location: our homes and families;

Vocation: our workplace;

Recreation: our rest and the places we play, relax, or unwind;

Restoration: where there is need; and

Multiplication: wherever else God may be calling us to go, even to the ends of the earth.

Throughout the book, we'll attempt to roll out each of these aspects, identities, and locations like a map, showing some of the ways they connect. Maps aren't just informational, though; they're invitational, too. They invite us to put boots on and see what the landscape looks like on the other side of that ridge or across the creek. They invite us to explore, to see, to get our hands dirty in unknown soil.

Likewise, we want to invite you to put your boots on and explore the world that's been formed and transformed by Jesus. Each chapter will end with a "Map It" section that serves as our invitation to you.

In part 1, looking at "The Whole Gospel," each chapter ends by zooming in and zooming out—looking at each gospel aspect from a broad and up-close perspective. These aspects aren't different maps, but three ways of looking at the same map, much as the map on your phone might offer a satellite view, a road view, or a hybrid view of the same terrain. By zooming out, we can look at the broad implications of that gospel aspect, and by zooming in, we can see the aspect's personal, immediate implications. Each Map It section ends by suggesting a passage of Scripture to pray through and meditate upon.

In part 2, "The Whole Church," we are looking at ways of living in the world formed by the gospel. So each identity is like a pathway through the world. When looking at a map this way, we need to know the answer to three questions: Where am I? Where am I going? How do I get there?

If we're looking at a map for our spiritual journey, in the light of the gospel, we need to ask three similar questions: Who am I? Where am I? How do I start?

Who Am I? The gospel transforms us from the inside out, giving us a radically new identity. Our way forward begins with understanding who God has transformed us to be.

Where Am I? Our next question is about defining us in relationship to what God has done. We need to honestly assess where we are in relationship with the landscape that he's created. If we're traveling from Louisville, Kentucky, to Portland, Oregon, we need to honestly acknowledge that our trip begins in Louisville, and not in Denver, Colorado. Pretending we're in Denver might provide a temporary and false assurance that our journey can be accomplished in one day of driving, but eventually, reality will catch up with us.

How Do I Start? As we look at what God has done and honestly assess where we stand in relationship to him, we can begin to discern our next step.

Part 3, "The Whole World," is all about making practical connections between the gospel and the world you inhabit. Your world is where your journey as a worshiper, family member, servant, disciple, and missionary gets practical. When that world collides with the gospel, great things happen. As Bilbo Baggins once told his nephew, "It's a dangerous business, going out your front door. You step on the road, and if you don't keep your feet, there's no telling where you'll be carried off to."[10]

Our spiritual journey is just such an unpredictable adventure. For two thousand years, Christians have explored the geography of the gospel, and it's compelled them off on unexpected journeys of all sorts. There's no predicting where God may lead you once you've come to discover the wonder of all he's done (and all he's yet to do) in Jesus. But that journey begins with a single step.

That step will be different for each of you. It's our hope that you'll explore this book prayerfully, and as you find yourself feeling invited, you'll wander down this or that byway. Feel free to simply explore the book leisurely, bouncing from this chapter to that one. There's a certain logic to the order of the chapters, but it's not essential that you read them that way.

After all, we're not making a map to take us from our house to the convenience store; we're making a map for the rest of our lives, opening up a gospel-transformed world that will be our home for eternity.

Faithmapping's goal is to show how the gospel, the church, and our mission are a coherent, organic, interrelated whole, rather than distinct, independent ideas. They inform and expand our understanding of each other, a whole gospel for a whole church on mission in the whole world.

Part One

The Whole Gospel

1

The Gospel of the Kingdom

For Jesus, the word "kingdom" meant
"God's dream for this world come true."

SCOT MCKNIGHT

The gospel of God's kingdom is the life with God under the rule of our King, Jesus. This life is announced by Jesus and made available through Jesus to all people. Simply put, the kingdom of God is the good life in Jesus.

Unfortunately, this is a foreign concept to most of us in the United States. With our national heritage of independence and rebellion, a suspicion of kings and aristocracy runs deep. In Hollywood, kings tend to fall in one of two categories: the Disney king, a charming, but generally dopey character (see *The Princess Bride* or *Sleeping Beauty*) or the tyrant. The tyrant, it seems, has much more appeal at the box office. Heroes like William Wallace in *Braveheart* lead a rebellion against the crown; Russell Crowe's gladiator eventually defeats Joaquin Phoenix's Caesar (who is both dumb and tyrannical). This is the place of the king in the modern American imagination.

Most of the actual monarchies remaining in the world are appropriately vilified for their very real tyranny. The Western world's most notable monarchy—the British Crown—while certainly not tyrannical, is more the focus of gossip and tabloid journalism than an object of our hopes and dreams. Our day-to-day lives are far removed from the kinds of kingdoms known in fairy tales and Bible stories. Theologian Russell Moore describes our dilemma well:

The Whole Gospel

> Most of us in the Western world have seen parodies of kings and crowns and kingdoms, but we've never seen anything approaching the real thing. So the language void is filled with all the chatter around us about the Prince of Wales or the local high school homecoming queen or the advertising slogans of the "king of beers" or the "Dairy Queen."[1]

It's no wonder, then, that the language of the "kingdom of God" fails to move us beyond confusion, glazed-over faces, mild nostalgia, or genuine revulsion. The concept of "kingdom" is far removed from both daily life and hopeful imagination.

The Gospel: A Kingdom Announcement

For Jesus and the writers of the New Testament, a "kingdom" was a real-life thing, something they encountered daily. It wasn't an abstract concept or a history lesson. They lived their lives under the absolute rule of Caesar, but Jesus announced that a new kingdom had arrived: life with God, under the rule of God, is made immediately available to us through the life and work of King Jesus.[2] Jesus's use of kingdom language was not simply poetic; it was a scandalous reality that got him killed.

The very word "gospel" has kingdom connotations. A "gospel" sent out in the Roman world was an important announcement related to the king—a celebration, an accession, or newly conquered land.[3]

British theologian N. T. Wright invites us to imagine what it must have been like to hear Jesus's message in the Roman world:

> Imagine what it would be like, in Britain or the United States today, if, without an election or any other official mechanism for changing the government, someone were to go on national radio and television and announce that there was now a new prime minister or president. "From today onward," says the announcer, "we have a new ruler! We're under new government! It's all going to be different!" That's not only exciting talk. It's fighting talk. It's treason! It's sedition! By what right is this man saying this? How does he think he'll get away with it? What exactly does he mean, anyway? An announcement like this isn't simply a proclamation. It's the start of a campaign. When a regime is already in power and is simply transferring that power to the next

person in line, you just announce that it's happening. But if you make that announcement while someone else appears to be in charge, you are saying, in effect, "The campaign starts here."⁴

The use of the word "gospel" by the writers of the New Testament was no accident. It was just such a declaration; there is a new kingdom where life with God is available under the rule of Jesus, our new King.

A World Full of Kingdoms

Though we might primarily associate monarchy with fairy tales and movies, kingdoms are an everyday reality. We live in a world of kingdoms, most of which are oppressive and self-serving. A kingdom can be defined as "the range of our effective will" or the place in which "what we want done gets done."⁵ In this sense, there are kingdoms all around us. They begin with our will. God created us with the power to rule over and subdue the earth (Gen. 1:26–28). We were not only made to live under God's rule; we were made to rule. That means that we have the power to extend the range of our will over the creation around us. We can make plants grow in straight rows, and shape creation into things like houses and iPhones. As we exercise our will, we impose our "rule" over the things around us, to varying effects. Sin's corruption has turned the creative power that was meant to glorify God into a power that seeks to glorify self.

We learn to exercise this power at a very young age, when we discover our autonomy and our ability to push our will over and against our parents or siblings. As any exhausted parent knows, the "no" of a two-year-old is a powerful thing. With any family battle, whether it's over cookies or curfews, it's a clash of kingdoms, and ultimately one must prevail.

The principle unfolds throughout our lives. We learn to exercise our wills and command our little kingdoms as we grow into adults. Men love to talk about how they're the "king of the castle," and in a limited sense, it's true. We rule over a little part of creation, and sometimes we have subjects who submit to our rule in business, family, and friendships. Some friends are "in charge" of their relationships, and that can be for evil as well as good.

Our tendency is to take whatever power we have and leverage it for whatever purpose suits us. Think of the influence one student can have in a classroom, or how one player can radically transform the effectiveness of a team. What would the Beatles have been without Paul or John? Consider the influence individual family members have on interpersonal dynamics during the holidays. Personal willpower, personal "kingdoms," assert tremendous and wide-ranging influence, and that influence can easily be for evil.

Beyond our smaller, personal kingdoms are the more obvious institutional kingdoms; governments, corporations, and various kinds of loyalties and obligations bind us to a set of rules and beliefs. These kingdoms overlap and intersect with one another, causing conflicts big and small. Our boss wants us to work longer hours and "get it done," while our family wants us to be more present at home. The internal conflict rages; what do you sacrifice, your career or your family?

Around the world, these conflicts are often far more direct. Corrupt governments put enormous pressure on citizens, crushing individual freedom. To someone in the Western world, word of a new "kingdom" sounds suspicious. To someone in Tibet, or Nigeria, it sounds like hope.

The Dark Kingdom

There's yet another kingdom that needs to be exposed. The book of Ephesians describes its ruler as the "prince of the power of the air," and talks about the "rulers," "authorities," and "cosmic powers over this present darkness" (2:2; 6:12). It's a kingdom that covers the earth and whose mission is to kill, steal, and destroy everything God has made (John 10:10). We see its fingerprints in global hunger and conflict, in AIDS epidemics and cancer wards, in death camps and terrorist camps. It's the kingdom of Satan, hell-bent on spreading lies, disease, and death, and it's all around us.

Of all the established kingdoms, this is the one at the root of evil in all the others. The evil king of that kingdom staked a claim in the human heart with Adam and Eve, and that curse has been passed down generation after generation. It's the reason we all are petty tyrants, and it's the reason we see bodies stacked like cordwood in Auschwitz and Rwanda. It has a death-grip on the world, simultaneously enslaving us and blinding us to our enslavement. We think we're free. We're not.

This kingdom's haunting presence—felt but not seen, experienced but not understood—makes films like *The Matrix* or *The Truman Show* ring true. We all have a sense that we're trapped and enslaved, that somehow we're not our own, but we lack the ability to see what snares us.

Hope for a Better King

We're left with a vague sense that the world isn't the way it's supposed to be, and we have a desire to see it made right. That energy gets channeled into all kinds of human effort, and movements emerge that promise a renewed and restored world through the cause-of-the-week: veganism, naturalism, capitalism, globalism, antiglobalism, racism, ageism, sexism, etc., etc.

Most powerfully, that energy emerges in the soaring rhetoric of politicians, who offer the hope of renewal and restoration. Our four-year cycle of presidential elections starts as a parade of impossible promises, and if you allow yourself to believe the rhetoric, you'll believe that an institution as massive as our government can change overnight . . . if we just elect the right person.

The public eats up these vain and hollow promises, filling yards and bumpers with slogans and symbols, hanging on the words of a cast of talking heads who spew rhetoric and propaganda during every election. Despite the deep frustration of the public, the cycle remains the same. In spite of our cynicism, an idealistic streak remains. We're simultaneously skeptics and true-believers because we know something's wrong with the world, and we believe that the right leader, the right king, could fix it. Richard Lovelace says, "In the hearts of the people is a groping, inarticulate conviction that, if the right ruler would only come along, the world would be healed of all its wounds. Creation is headless and desperately searching for its head."[6] This is the predicament of our world: a competing cacophony of kingdoms and power-mongering, all ruled over by Satan himself, the evil old king whose end goal is death and decay. Humanity is trapped under an oppressive ruler, blind to his control, and blind to its own spiritual blindness. We jockey for power, we bicker and fight, we wage war politically and economically, and we watch with hope for someone who can set us free.

The Kingdom Announced by Jesus

Into that madness comes Jesus of Nazareth. After lying low for thirty years, Jesus began a public ministry with words that slice right through the chaos of the world's kingdoms: "The time is fulfilled, and the kingdom of God is at hand; repent and believe in the gospel" (Mark 1:15).

It's important to notice that the gospel is not simply an invitation; it's a declaration, an announcement: The time has come for God to be your king. He's reclaiming and restoring his world. Repent of all of your petty kingdoms and believe this good news. It's a declaration of war against the competing claims for authority, and it's an invasion of God's power and rule. Remember—a kingdom is where what the king wants done, gets done. So God's kingdom is where what God wants done gets done. The life of Jesus as displayed in the Gospels shows that kingdom invading and transforming the order of the world, declaring war on the petty political and religious kingdoms that surround us, and on the old king's reign of death and destruction.

In the verses that follow Jesus's announcement in Mark 1:15, he calls his followers and begins his public ministry. Jesus's early ministry is a vivid image of the kingdom invading. He's healing the sick, casting out demons, and cleansing lepers—a direct assault on sickness and death. Jesus's healing ministry is one of his most direct assaults on the evil king's order. Sickness and death are abundant in our fallen and broken world, and we need to constantly remind ourselves that it wasn't meant to be this way. The world wasn't meant to be pock-marked with hospitals and clinics, TB wards and ghettos populated with sick, crippled, starving, and forgotten people. Their presence is a constant reminder of the evil king's rule.

When Jesus announces the kingdom and begins to heal the sick, rescue people from the brink of death, and cast out demons, we see what this kingdom is all about. He goes to what Tim Keller calls the "spoiling places" of the world, showing how God intends to reverse the curse and redeem the world. The arrival of God's kingdom means that death and decay aren't going to have the final victory, and Jesus's ministry shows the enemies retreating. Demons flee. Disease heals. Death is held at bay. In the beginning of John's Gospel, he describes Jesus's arrival: "The light shines in the darkness, and the darkness has not overcome it" (John 1:5).

The gospel of the kingdom is the announcement that life with God, under the rule of God, is made immediately available to us through Jesus, our King. He arrives as one who restores, rules, and provides access to God's kingdom.

A Kingdom Restored by Jesus

This is actually not the beginning of something new, but the restoration of something very old, something that was long lost. We were actually created for the good life. We were created to live our days filled with joy, satisfaction, and celebration. God's world was once a joy-filled harmony, filled with the glory of God and unstained by sin in all of its dark manifestations.

The clearest picture we have is in Genesis 1 and 2 where we see a world without gossip and slander, without pain and disease, without envy or pride or war or murder. We were created as God's image-bearers, and we were meant to live in harmony with God and with one another. This means that everything—how we worked, how we lived, how we loved, how we ate—everything we did was to reflect who God is and how he designed life to work. The Bible shows us that this all came apart when sin entered the world. The Serpent tempts

Eve, and Eve invites Adam into her sin. Sin declares war on God's rule, introducing chaos and disorder to the perfect harmony he'd made. With it comes a world at war against us (Gen. 3:17–18), and humanity at war with itself (Gen. 3:16). In the midst of this newfound chaos, God promises a Redeemer, One born of a woman who will crush the Serpent that introduced this evil to the world (Gen. 3:15). That divine promise is why the world obsessively looks for a hero—political or otherwise—who might once and for all make things right.

The story that unfolds shows God patiently leading human history toward the moment that Jesus arrives. He gets little help from his people. The rhythm of the Old Testament is one in which God establishes a covenant, the covenant is broken, the people suffer and repent, and God restores them. Again. And again. And again. From a human perspective, it's an imperfect arrangement. No one in the whole story of the Old Testament seems to be able to keep his hands pure. When you read the genealogies of Jesus in the book of Luke, it's a long list of miscreants, swindlers, and ne'er-do-wells. But God is orchestrating history on a march toward Jesus. Throughout the story, there are hints and whispers of a coming King who will fix it all. The prophet Isaiah paints a picture of that hope when he says:

> The Spirit of the Lord GOD is upon me,
>   because the LORD has anointed me
> to bring good news to the poor;
>   he has sent me to bind up the brokenhearted,
> to proclaim liberty to the captives,
>   and the opening of the prison to those who are bound;
> to proclaim the year of the LORD's favor. (Isa. 61:1–2)

It's an affirmation of something we intuitively feel. The world isn't as it should be: we weren't created for ashes; we were made for beauty. We weren't created for sadness and suffering, we were made for joy and gladness. God is essentially saying, "Something far better is coming. If you feel crushed and broken, don't despair, because the world isn't how it's meant to be, and isn't how it's going to be."

A Kingdom Made Available through Jesus

Seven hundred years later, Jesus walks into a synagogue and reads the opening lines of the above passage. He then turns to the congregation and says, "Today this scripture has been fulfilled in your hearing" (Luke 4:21). This is a bombshell. Israel was under the thumb of the Romans, and her former glory was gone. "The year of the LORD's favor" was a promise of restoration: God is going to come back to us, and life with God will be available to us again. But for Jesus to declare this in first-century Israel would be like someone walking into a community center in China and declaring himself the new emperor, announcing an end to oppression and suffering. The response of the crowd reveals how scandalous his announcement was. They tried to kill him on the spot.

When Jesus says, "The Spirit of the Lord GOD is upon me," he's claiming spectacular authority. The crowds get excited about the Jesus who heals the sick and turns back death; it's the moment he announces his authority and his intentions that they start to get angry. They see miracles and ask for more, but Jesus responds by telling us that they're just a hint of what he's doing, that the core of what he's doing is rewriting history. He's on a mission, and his miracles are mere glimpses of his authority and power.

His authority was foretold from the time of his conception. An angel told Mary, "He will be great and will be called the Son of the Most High. And the Lord God will give to him the throne of his father David, and he will reign over the house of Jacob forever, and of his kingdom there will be no end" (Luke 1:32–33). He's the heir to David's throne, anointed with the Spirit of God, sent to announce this good news, this gospel of God's kingdom.

During Jesus's lifetime, he's humbled. He lives a quiet life for thirty years, and even in the midst of his public ministry, he runs the gamut from being welcomed by adoring crowds to being the object of insult and threats. Ultimately, his claims to authority lead him to the humiliation of the cross, but this is all part of God's plan.[7] As Paul tells us, "For our sake he made him to be sin who knew no sin, so that in him we might become the righteousness of God" (2 Cor. 5:21).

It's an incredible plan. The ruler of the kingdom suffers for the subjects. He humbles himself and lives among them, suffering under the same injustice, encountering the same competing kingdoms. Jesus encountered the authority of the kingdoms around him, all the while preaching that God's kingdom was here, and was greater than all these others. He suffered under Pilate's kingdom. He suffered under religious corruption—a kind of kingdom. He suffered under Satan's kingdom, subject even to death. Yet, in humbling himself, he flips the whole world on its head, and this crucified and downtrodden One becomes the name exalted above every name.

It didn't have to be this way. God could have established his kingdom again without the suffering of Jesus, returning to rule over creation. The result would have been a world without mercy, and there would have been no hope for us. God, in his great love for his people, sacrificed Jesus to make a way for sinners to come back into his kingdom. Through the cross, God has given us an all-access pass behind the curtain, an open invitation to his life-giving presence. (We'll have much more to say about the cross in the next chapter.)

Jesus's humiliating victory is what opens the door of the kingdom for all of us. It should sound scandalous, bizarre, and weird. Our familiarity with this message breeds a complacent, casual response, when the Bible indicates it should be all but that. It's one thing for a king to die for his people. It's another for him to die for rebels. But he did, and his end game was to welcome us into the kingdom, to welcome us into life lived in communion with God. It's God's "good pleasure" to give us the kingdom (Luke 12:32). It's his joy to restore life to the dying world.

The gospel is an announcement of a wartime victory. God has conquered our old, tyrannical enemies, at the cross and empty tomb, and he is leading a conspiracy of rebellion against the old king's grip upon our world. Through Jesus, and through Jesus's people (the church), the tide is changing, and all of the enemies will be finished, including death (1 Cor. 15:25–27).

Responding to the King's Invitation: Repent and Believe

The gospel of God's kingdom is the announcement that life with God is available to all who put their faith in the life, death, and resurrection of Jesus. Against the Serpent's kingdom, government and corporate kingdoms, and our own individual kingdoms stands the kingdom of God, where Jesus is King. In his kingdom, what he wants done gets done. In his kingdom, life works the way he designed it to. His kingdom is not ruled by sin, by human greed or corruption, but rather by the One who is turning back darkness, reversing the curse, and making all things new.

Citizenship in the modern world requires much of us. Applying for citizenship requires classes and screenings and tests. Being a citizen requires paying taxes and obeying the law of the land. Yet the gospel is extended as a gift. What God demands—perfect obedience—he provides in Jesus. Citizenship in his kingdom doesn't require us to live up to God's high standards to gain entry. The good news, the announcement of the gospel, is that this gift is available to us for free, by the declaration of the new King.

What it requires, then, is a response. When Jesus appears on the scene in Mark 1 and makes his announcement, he uses two words to describe the necessary response of his listeners: repent and believe.

These words have often been used in ways that have obscured and confused their simple meaning. When we hear "repent," we often think of obnoxious televangelists, or tracts left out in restaurants or bathrooms with words in bold, block letters. It evokes images of self-punishment, of suffering and struggling against temptation. "Believe" has had its own share of abuses, evoking a vision of Christianity where salvation is about a heavenly entrance exam. If we can just get the answers right, so long as we "believe" this stuff, we get in. So we need some help in hearing these words afresh, as Jesus's original audience would have.

The Whole Gospel

So what, then, does it mean to repent?

To repent means to turn away from something and to turn toward something else. It means a reshaping of our mindset, a new way of looking at the world. It means rethinking our way of thinking and being and doing. We currently live in service of a variety of kingdoms: our personal kingdom; our family's kingdom, perhaps our business or political kingdom, and unbeknownst to most of us, we are subject to the evil king and his kingdom of darkness. His power in the world and in our hearts has caused us to live a life of resistance, rebellion, and denial of God's authority. When we repent, we not only acknowledge that reality, we change our allegiance. To be part of a kingdom means to have loyalty for a king. Repentance is a transformation of our loyalties, from a world of idols to the one true King. Paul praised this kind of transformation being reported in the Thessalonian church when he told them of their reputation for "how you turned to God from idols to serve the living and true God" (1 Thess. 1:9).

Repentance means facing the reality of our sinful alliance with these smaller kingdoms, turning away from them, and turning toward the greater kingdom revealed in Jesus Christ. It means looking at our orientation toward the world and toward our selves, acknowledging that it's all been stained and corrupted by sin. We're deeply broken, and our hearts are sold into captivity to evil, twisted, selfish kingdoms.

Intertwined with repentance is belief. Repenting requires belief, and belief results in repentance. Another way to think about belief is to think in terms of faith. Faith is simply seeing, believing, and embracing who Jesus is, what he has done, and all that he promises to do. As we see Jesus, as we come to believe that his kingdom is the prize and power he says it is, we will irresistibly turn away from these other loyalties. What he offers surpasses the hopes and promises of this fading world.

We often think that this is all pain and drudgery. We think repentance is something that we have to scrape and claw our way through, and we hope we'll come out the other side a changed person. But Jesus doesn't paint the picture that way. In fact, if we look at the way he describes the kingdom of God, any pain and drudgery would come from missing out on the chance to enter it.

Reimagining Repentance

Jesus describes repentance like this:

> The kingdom of heaven is like treasure hidden in a field, which a man found and covered up. Then in his joy he goes and sells all that he has and buys that field.
>
> Again, the kingdom of heaven is like a merchant in search of fine pearls, who on finding one pearl of great value, went and sold all that he had and bought it. (Matt. 13:44–46)

Let's imagine this in modern terms. Picture a broke college student who walked through a vacant lot in his neighborhood. As he passed through, he tripped over something protruding out of the ground. Intrigued, he did a little digging. He worked through the sod and clay until he discovered an old steamer trunk, buried in what would have once been someone's backyard (the house had been long-demolished). Inside were stacks and stacks of government bonds, which have quietly gained a mountain of interest over seven or eight decades. It was worth a fortune. There was enough information to tie it to the property, so someone couldn't just walk away with it. It belonged in this yard, and the owners of the land had rights to it. But the property was for sale.

Acting quickly, the student rushed home, listed his whole apartment's worth of belongings on Craigslist and eBay, sold his broken-down Volvo, his brand-new MacBook and iPhone, his clothes, his stereo, his Xbox, and his plasma TV to come up with the $15,000 cash to buy the vacant lot. The deal was sealed a few weeks later, and he cashed in the bonds for an incredible fortune.

Let that scene define the word "repent" for you. Surely, friends of the college student (or the treasure hunter) thought he was crazy. "Surely," they thought, "he's lost his mind. He's getting rid of *everything*?"

But to the person in the know, there's a wonderful economy at work here. The loss of the young man's belongings paled in comparison to the gain of the bonds. What he lost was worth far, far less than what he gained. In the economy of the kingdom of God, repentance means a loss of these lesser things that have our hearts, laying off our addiction to sin and self, but gaining life with God, the life we were made for. The man in Jesus's parable, or our college student, has faith because he knows that buried underground is a hope beyond his dreams, a wildly extravagant treasure that makes him willing to sacrifice everything because of its surpassing worth.

To the person with faith, the only thing that's absurd is to abandon the opportunity set before him, the opportunity to experience the riches of the gospel. Something so good and rich is laid before us, and it promises to satisfy the aching and longing of our hearts. The glory of the one far outweighs the other, and no cost is too great.

This is a seismic shift in the way that we see the world. If we can get a glimpse of the glory of the kingdom of God and the glory of our King, there should be an irrepressible response to chase after it with all that we have. It's an unimaginable opportunity—far greater than buried treasure.

This is a stark contrast to the way we tend to think about how people change. We tend to think much more in terms of struggle and discipline, like going to boot camp or doing our taxes. Author Garrison Keillor once said that a monogamous man is like a bear riding a tricycle; he can do it, but he'd much rather be out in the woods.[8] That's how we feel about much of the Christian life; it can be done, but we'd rather be doing something else.

But the kingdom metaphors paint a totally different picture. The motivation comes once someone glimpses the kingdom. The real pain, the real drudgery, would be to miss out on the opportunity to enter it.

It's helpful to come back to the idea of the gospel as an announcement. Fundamentally, this message is not about something we do, but what God has done. It's an announcement made to anyone and everyone: Life with God is available now through Jesus Christ. It's an indictment and an invitation. It indicts us for serving lesser kingdoms, and it offers an invitation to the life we've always longed for.

The kingdom is offered as a gift. It's a life that's overflowing with God's own joy and goodness. We have a new King, not because we've earned something (through our good works or obedience) but because he's conquered us, and he's conquered the enemies that surround us. To repent and believe means that we see that old kingdom for what it is—a dark, dying thing—and switch our allegiance. Where once we served and lived for this other kingdom, now we live for our new King.

There's a scene relived in many of the old tales of knights and kings. When the old king breathes his last, all eyes turn to the next in line for succession. Someone inevitably says, "The king is dead," to which the others, looking at the new king, reply, "Long live the king!"

The old evil king is dead. Since Adam, he's ruled over our entire globe, extending a fierce mechanism of death, disease, and decay. Jesus has conquered the old king, stripped him of his power, and exposed him to the world. The king is dead. Long live the King.

Map It

Q. What is the gospel of the kingdom?

A: It is the good news that life with God under the rule of God is available to all who would turn from their rebellion and trust in King Jesus.

Zoom Out

The Bible is filled with God calling us back into life with him. It's the story of God creating his kingdom, us being expelled from his kingdom, and God promising to restore us back into his kingdom. As you read, look for God's invitations and promises about life under his good rule. God's presence—in the stories, in the Psalms, in the promises of the prophets—is evidence of God's kingdom slowly breaking into the world.

Zoom In

The parables of Jesus show the kingdom as a life-changing personal discovery. Consider meditating on a few of them:

The Whole Gospel

- Entering God's Kingdom (Matt. 20:1–16; Luke 12:13–21)
- Growing in God's Kingdom (Matt. 13:31–33; Mark 4:26–29)
- Living in God's Kingdom (Luke 10:25–37; 15:11–32)[9]

Pray It: Matthew 6:9–13

> Our Father in heaven,
> hallowed be your name.
> Your kingdom come,
> your will be done,
> > on earth as it is in heaven.
> Give us this day our daily bread,
> and forgive us our debts,
> > as we also have forgiven our debtors.
> And lead us not into temptation,
> > but deliver us from evil. (Matt. 6:9–13)

2

The Gospel of the Cross

What could a child know of the darkness of God's plan?

CORMAC MCCARTHY

Man, in his natural spirit of self-justifying legalism, has tried to get away
from the cross of Christ and its perfection, or to erect another cross
instead, or to set up a screen of ornaments between himself and it,
or to alter its true meaning into something more congenial to his tastes,
or to transfer the virtue of it to some act or performance or feeling
of its own. Thus the simplicity of the cross is nullified, and its
saving power is denied. For the cross saves completely, or not at all.

HORATIUS BONAR

Imagine if a young child came into a preschool class wearing a colorful, screen-printed pastel T-shirt. In the background was a shining sun
and a rainbow, spilling light onto a field of flowers and greenery. In
the foreground, lit up by that light and happiness, was a hangman's
noose. Or an electric chair. Or perhaps, a man with a hood tied over
his head, standing in front of a firing squad or being waterboarded.

You would probably call Child Protective Services.

The Roman Cross

For someone who lived in the Roman Empire, the image of the cross
would evoke similar emotions. Throughout the empire, it was an
unmistakable image of criminality, guilt, and shame. Crucifixion
was a horrible and cruel means of death, wherein the one crucified

was spiked through the hands and feet and suspended onto wooden crossbeams. Beyond the agony of the wounds, the posture constricted breathing. The criminal would then be forced to pull himself up on the spikes through his hands and push up from his pierced feet in order to take a breath. Death didn't come from bleeding, though criminals were often beaten or flogged before their crucifixion and blood was abundant. It came through asphyxiation, as the pain of breathing became too great a burden for the body to bear. It could take hours or even days to die.

Crucifixion was used in Rome as a public means of execution, putting on display the price that lawbreakers who dared defy the Roman Empire would pay. Bodies would be left to rot on crosses along roadways and in public places, to both shame the criminal and warn the populace. Cicero, a Roman philosopher and orator who lived from 106–43 BC, found the use of the cross disgusting, inhumane, and beneath the dignity of Roman citizens. He said that the very word "cross," should "be far removed from not only the bodies of Roman citizens but even from their thoughts, their eyes, and their ears."[1]

Graffiti from those days shows Christ on the cross with the head of a donkey. Christians were seen by the Roman world as fools who worshiped an ass on the cross.[2] It's this sense of revulsion and disgust that informs the apostle Paul's words in 1 Corinthians, where he says: "The word of the cross is folly to those who are perishing, but to us who are being saved it is the power of God" (1 Cor. 1:18). And later: "I decided to know nothing among you except Jesus Christ and him crucified" (1 Cor. 2:2).

Paul centered his work and ministry on the grotesque image and message of a crucified Savior. This should alert us to the profound centrality of the cross to the message of the gospel. *The gospel of God's cross is the good news that, through the life, death, and resurrection of Jesus, we have been made right with God.*[3] If the kingdom of God is a map defined by expanding borders and victory at war, the map defined by the cross is a blood-stained map, marked by suffering and tragedy.

Denying the Cross

For some reason, the human heart gravitates away from that message. We would prefer a simpler means of salvation, something not so violent, perhaps, or so shameful. Maybe that's why we turn the image of the cross into a trinket, or why we look for alternatives.

Jesus witnessed this tendency in his disciples:

> And he began to teach them that the Son of Man must suffer many things and be rejected by the elders and the chief priests and the scribes and be killed, and after three days rise again. And he said this plainly. And Peter took him aside and began to rebuke him. But turning and seeing his disciples, he rebuked Peter and said, "Get behind me, Satan! For you are not setting your mind on the things of God, but on the things of man." (Mark 8:31–33)

As Jesus had gone about his mission, healing the sick, rebuking the self-righteous, and spreading the message of God's kingdom, Peter and many others had missed the point. They saw Jesus's displays of power as a catalyst for a political movement—a force that would arrive to transform the world and put Israel at its center, with Jesus as its king. Their vision wasn't too grand; it was too narrow. The stranglehold of the Romans on Israel was nothing compared to the stranglehold of Satan, sin, and death, and Jesus knew that conquering them would require an ultimate act of sacrifice. For Jesus to crush the Serpent, he must first feel his sting.

Peter is horrified. As we can see from other passages, his hopes aren't merely for the redemption of Israel, but for his own heightened stature in a kingdom where Jesus is king. A few verses earlier, we see Jesus ask his disciples who they think he is. Peter responds, "You are the Christ," and Jesus praises him for recognizing it. In the parallel passage in Matthew, Jesus responds to Peter's confession by saying:

> Blessed are you, Simon Bar-Jonah! For flesh and blood has not revealed this to you, but my Father who is in heaven. And I tell you, you are Peter, and on this rock I will build my church, and the gates of hell shall not prevail against it. I will give you the keys of the kingdom of heaven, and whatever you bind on earth shall be bound in

heaven, and whatever you loose on earth shall be loosed in heaven. (Matt. 16:17–19)

Moments later comes this stunning rebuke, "Get behind me, Satan!" This sounds crazy. One moment, he's telling Peter that he's brilliant, the next he calls him Satan. But Jesus isn't merely being moody.

He affirms Peter's confession and rebukes him moments later because he's reframing his followers' understanding of his mission. This actually happens several times in Mark 8–10. After rebuking Peter, he says, "If anyone would come after me, let him deny himself and take up his cross and follow me. For whoever would save his life will lose it, but whoever loses his life for my sake and the gospel's will save it" (Mark 8:34–35). This actually happens two more times in Mark 8–10. In Mark 9, the disciples are having an argument about who will be the greatest in Jesus's kingdom when he establishes his reign, and Jesus responds by saying, "If anyone would be first, he must be last of all and servant of all" (Mark 9:35).

In Mark 10:35–37, James and John pull Jesus aside and ask for the right to sit on either side of him when he ascends his throne. You can just imagine the frustration for Jesus, who knows that the cross is ahead of him, and who has been calling these men to humble themselves and prepare for service, sacrifice, and even death. "You do not know what you're asking," he says (v. 38). To ask to share in Jesus's glory was to ask to share in his suffering—something they'd both experience after the resurrection. The other disciples get angry because they too don't get it—they think he's offering them power and glory, when in fact he's inviting them to experience the agony of persecution.

Jesus is preparing them for the great shock of his incarnation: the cross. He was born to die. After watching the powers of hell flee from him, seeing darkness turn to light, witnessing the oppressive religious leaders of the day stunned into silence, they knew he had some serious power. They couldn't imagine why he'd allow himself to be chained, beaten, and hung on a cross.

Cross Denial throughout History

Peter's horror at Jesus's march to the cross is a foreshadow of the way many have responded to the cross for centuries. You can see in Peter why some have come to try to separate the gospel of God's kingdom and the gospel of God's cross. For some, the gospel of the kingdom is an attractive message: life with God is available to us again. If you really understand what it means, it's like winning the lottery, and who wouldn't want that? But when the cross—with its bloody imagery and with talk of sin and punishment—becomes a part of the conversation, people begin to dismiss it as foolish and primitive.[4]

Throughout the centuries, there have been Christians who've sought to deny that imagery, or sideline it. Revivalist Charles Finney, for instance, referred to the idea that Jesus's death on the cross was a substitute for us and a payment for our sins as a "theological fiction."[5] Contemporary pastor and author Steve Chalke once referred to the wrath-atoning death of Jesus as a case of "cosmic child abuse."[6] Less sinister (but no less harmful) examples exist, like those who preach about a life of blessing and life with God, but never deal with the sinful conditions that pervade our world.

It is tempting for Christians to preach a gospel that doesn't deal with sin, and doesn't require the cross. It is tempting to speak of life with God without addressing the realities of life without God, the kingdom of darkness, and the separation that exists between us. But the cross and the kingdom have such deep connections that they can't be separated without diminishing their power. N. T. Wright said, "It seems to me that a great gulf has been placed between Kingdom and Cross, but in Matthew, Mark, Luke and John, they go extremely closely together, and they are more or less defined in relation to one another."[7]

The Cross Promised

We said in the last chapter that the announcement of the kingdom isn't the announcement of something new, but the restoration of something very, very old. In Genesis 1 and 2, we see the tiniest glimpse of what a world without sin was like, and we know that this is the course toward which all of history is moving. But in Genesis 3 we see how it was lost, and why it needs restoration.

That story begins when Adam and Eve break the one command God gave them. Eve's temptation is to "be like God," an interesting sin. God made Eve, and he made her perfect. She was righteous, but in her sin, she felt that the righteousness and glory that God provided for her weren't enough. So she eats the forbidden fruit, hoping to become greater, and the world begins to unravel. Adam eats the fruit with her, and it spells both of their deaths. Ashamed, they rush to hide their sin, making inadequate fig leaf loincloths to attempt to restore their dignity.

God discovers them in their sin, and tells them what they've unleashed on the world:

The Lord God said to the serpent,

> "Because you have done this,
>   cursed are you above all livestock
>   and above all beasts of the field;
> on your belly you shall go,
>   and dust you shall eat
>   all the days of your life.
> I will put enmity between you and the woman,
>   and between your offspring and her offspring;
> he shall bruise your head,
>   and you shall bruise his heel."

To the woman he said,

> "I will surely multiply your pain in childbearing;
>   in pain you shall bring forth children.
> Your desire shall be for your husband,
>   and he shall rule over you."

And to Adam he said,

> "Because you have listened to the voice of your wife
>   and have eaten of the tree

of which I commanded you,
   'You shall not eat of it,'
cursed is the ground because of you;
   in pain you shall eat of it all the days of your life;
thorns and thistles it shall bring forth for you;
   and you shall eat the plants of the field.
By the sweat of your face
   you shall eat bread,
till you return to the ground,
   for out of it you were taken;
for you are dust,
   and to dust you shall return."

The man called his wife's name Eve, because she was the mother of all living. And the Lord God made for Adam and for his wife garments of skins and clothed them. (Gen. 3:14–21)

Notice there's a great deal of suffering predicted in this passage. Thorns, thistles, sweat, and dust are now part of Adam and Eve's future. Childbearing and marriage are now marked by pain and disunity. Work is now laborious, and death is a new and present reality. Sin has entered the world, twisting the goodness and harmony in which it was made into something menacing and deadly.

But there's a glimmer of hope in the midst of this profound suffering—a promise of glory. First, God tells the Serpent that though he'll strike the heel of Eve's offspring, that offspring will strike his head. In other words, through Eve will come someone to finish off the Serpent. It's both a promise of suffering (the struck heel) and glory (the crushed Serpent).

Second, God replaces the insufficient fig leaves with skins. He takes his naked, disgraced children, and dresses them. It's like a father, discovering his runaway child—bruised, filthy, and ashamed—and cleaning him, bandaging him, and clothing him. Our efforts to cover our sins are like those fig leaves, shoddy and flimsy. We need to be cleansed and clothed by our Father.

Notice how that happened. God didn't go to the Gap to buy their clothes. Something died to cover their disgrace. Adam and Eve were dressed in animal skins because their sin required bloodshed. God, who had every right to take offense, instead covered their shame. There is suffering—the death of a sacrifice—and glory—the restored dignity of God's people.

Throughout the Old Testament, this movement of suffering and glory is echoed again and again. Read Psalm 22, and watch how the psalm moves from the suffering of the Chosen One to the glory of the Chosen One, and the greater glory of God. The exodus story is a cyclical tale of suffering and glory: Moses narrowly escapes death as an infant, but rises to become a high-level political leader. Moses loses it all when he murders an Egyptian, but God calls him to be a leader for his people. Israel suffers as slaves, and is called out of Egypt. On and on the examples go.

This movement of suffering and glory seems to be at the heart of the biblical story, and all of the suffering in the Scriptures points us to the cross, where the suffering of God makes way for the surpassing glory of God to be put on display.

Crossless Christianity wants the glory without the suffering. It wants access to God (Genesis 2) without acknowledging the ravaging effects of sin in our hearts and in our world (Genesis 3). Jesus calls his followers to deny themselves and take up a cross; a share in the kingdom means a share in suffering. Paul shows us in Philippians 2 that Jesus's glory is put on display because of his willingness to suffer the humiliation of putting on human flesh and enduring death on the cross.

Our Cross-Hungry World

Those who would steer us toward a crossless Christianity have to ignore most of the Bible to get there, but they also have to ignore the pulse of the culture around us. Blood, suffering, and sacrifice play significant roles in the stories we tell in TV and movies. It's almost as though we instinctually know that redemption requires suffering, bloodshed, and death.

How boring would the Harry Potter book and movie series be

if Harry and his friends didn't have to endure suffering and death to defeat their enemy? It would be a nonstory, and it certainly wouldn't be an international phenomenon.

There is no small obsession with blood in North America today. There's the recent obsession with teenage vampires, where blood is the key to eternal life. There's *The Wrestler*, where Mickey Rourke's character—a past-his-prime Hulk Hogan–type—secretly cuts himself during wrestling matches to excite the crowd, making his matches more violent and keeping the crowd coming back. His girlfriend recites Isaiah 53 when remembering the stories: "He was pierced for our transgressions, he was wounded for our iniquities." With his life and career falling apart, he sheds his own blood in an effort at self-made redemption.

Perhaps the most disturbing example comes from *Dexter*, a show about a man who by day is a blood-spatter analyst for the Miami police, and by night is a serial killer whose victims are criminals who escaped the system. As monstrous as Dexter's crimes are, each of his victims is displayed for his or her own horrendousness. It's dark and disturbing; his lust for blood is depraved and perverse, and we should see it no other way. Yet he remains, in some small part, an antihero because we can't help but share his desire for justice for the victims of his victims.

The writers of the show aren't subtle at all about the atoning power of blood and death. The vast amounts of blood in the show are far more than a gory prop because blood remains a powerful symbol of sin, punishment, justice, and death. Dexter's whole life is surrounded by blood, marking his entire existence with its stain, weight, and meaning. As violent as the show is, I think at no point could you accuse it of taking life and death lightly.

Blood "Speaks"

All such blood and violence has its foreshadow in Genesis 4, where we see where sin will take the world. Cain and Abel both offer sacrifices to the Lord, but Cain's is not accepted. Cain then kills Abel. In a passage that's very relevant to a conversation about the cross, God comes to Cain and says:

> "Where is Abel your brother?" He said, "I do not know; am I my brother's keeper?" And the LORD said, "What have you done? The voice of your brother's blood is crying to me from the ground. And now you are cursed from the ground, which has opened its mouth to receive your brother's blood from your hand." (Gen. 4:9–11)

The fact that Abel's blood "speaks" is not insignificant. When we see bloodstains, they "speak." No one would walk into a room and see a pool of blood and feel at ease. No one would buy a car with blood-stained seats. Blood in TV, movies, and literature creates the same skin-crawling feeling. Blood speaks. It cries out, alerting us that something has gone terribly, tragically wrong.

Much could be said about the metaphors at work in *Dexter*, *Twilight*, and other shows that hinge upon bloodshed and hint at redemption, like *The Mentalist* or the film *True Grit*. I point them out here to illustrate the power that blood and sacrifice have in the modern imagination, even as some would have us remove such imagery from our faith. Something deep within us resonates with this imagery because it's true. Something is deeply wrong with the world, and we're looking for ways to set it right. In the imagination of many, blood seems to be a part of the answer. That's no coincidence.

When we abandon the cross and the shed blood of Jesus, we lose the ability to respond to that deep murmur in our hearts. The gospel makes no sense without its power. This is why Jesus responds so fiercely to Peter. He knows that there is no hope for glory and redemption apart from his own suffering and death. To conquer the Serpent, he must first feel his sting.

Avoiding the Cross—Avoiding Our Sin

Perhaps one reason the disciples (and we too) want the glory without the suffering is that we think too little of our sin. If sin is a minor problem, then perhaps God could simply show up and start reigning again.

The Scriptures tell us otherwise—sin, both in the world at large and at large in our hearts—is the great problem in the universe.

Isaiah had a vision of what the Messiah would do to reconcile a broken world and broken people to God. Seven hundred years before the crucifixion, he said of Jesus:

> Surely he has borne our griefs
> and carried our sorrows;
> yet we esteemed him stricken,
> smitten by God, and afflicted.
> But he was pierced for our transgressions;
> he was crushed for our iniquities;
> upon him was the chastisement that brought us peace,
> and with his wounds we are healed.
> All we like sheep have gone astray;
> we have turned—every one—to his own way;
> and the LORD has laid on him
> the iniquity of us all. (Isa. 53:4–6)

What Isaiah dreamed of, the promise that Adam and Eve heard in the garden, the foretaste that the Passover lamb illustrated in Egypt—all pointed to the cross. The cross is the long-awaited promise of God to cover our sin and shame.

Perhaps some Christians want to avoid the cross because it brings them face-to-face with their shame. Adam and Eve's fig leaves were an effort to say, "I'm still okay, I still have some dignity." Accepting God's animal skins required acknowledging how insufficient the fig leaves were. Had the disciples understood the cross during Jesus's lifetime, there would have been no arguments about "who's the greatest." The cross is an instrument of punishment for condemned criminals, and if we believe that Jesus went there in our place, we must believe that it's a death we deserve.

Some of us don't want to acknowledge that we deserve that punishment. We think we can do our best and earn God's approval. Most religions of the world are built around an economy wherein we obey and are accepted. In Islam, faithful participation in the habits of religion are the key to salvation. Hindus seek transcendence by pleasing their gods. Buddhists seek enlightenment from refining the habits of the mind. Like all the other religions of the world, we want to believe that we can do something—we want to believe that we can earn approval and pay the debt ourselves. But the cross shames those who refuse it, and looms large by displaying the cost of our sins. The Romans hung criminals at crossroads and byways to declare the price paid by those guilty of treason, and the crucified Savior hangs like just such a criminal, but declares that he's there in our place. The cross declares an end to earned approval before God, and calls us to a radical new way of acceptance: resting in Jesus's finished work. "Christ redeemed us from the curse of the law by becoming a curse for us—for it is written, 'Cursed is everyone who is hanged on a tree'" (Gal. 3:13).

The Bible is clear from front to back that we are incapable of repairing the rift between God and us, but the gospel of God's cross announces that it is Jesus's life, death, and resurrection that saves us from our sins and makes us right with God.

Isaiah 30:15 is helpful: "In repentance and rest is your salvation . . . but you would have none of it" (NIV). We refuse the offer of rest in Jesus's finished work because we refuse to believe what he says about our desperate state apart from him.

The Story of the Cross

It's only through the cross that we can experience the glory of the kingdom. The bloodstained map drawn by the cross shows us the only way to enter life with God—the life we desperately long for. Jesus's prediction doesn't end with his death; it ends with the promise of resurrection.

> And he began to teach them that the Son of Man must suffer many things and be rejected by the elders and the chief priests and the scribes and be killed, and after three days rise again. (Mark 8:31)

The cross would be a hopeless story if it weren't punctuated by the empty tomb. Jesus tells us that before his crucifixion. Paul tells us in 1 Corinthians 15 that if Christ isn't raised, we're to be pitied more than anyone on earth. The resurrection is the clearest way God can demonstrate to the world that death has no power over those who belong to Christ. But apart from a fully informed understanding of the depths of our sins, the wonder of the resurrection is diminished. Because we are great sinners, we need a great Savior, and the cross and resurrection are the proof that our sins are paid for and death is defeated.

When Jesus and the disciples come to Jerusalem, all of Christ's predictions come true. A crowd gathers when he enters the city, and the scene becomes raucous. It's less like one of our Palm Sunday services, with children and choirs waving palms and singing in harmony, and more like something we'd see on CNN. As author Reggie McNeal once provocatively described it, Jesus shows up in Jerusalem, steals a car, and starts a street riot.[8] The crowd, like the disciples, sees his power as something that can be leveraged against their Roman oppressors, but Jesus has his eyes on the bigger targets: sin and death.

Later, when he's betrayed, arrested, and on trial, that crowd turns against him. Perhaps it was his failure to rally a militia against Rome that made them so angry. Perhaps they simply believed the charges against him. Whatever the case, they called out, "Crucify him" (Mark 15:13–14). Jesus is flogged, beaten, spit upon, and led to Golgotha. Mark 15:25–26 reads, "And it was the third hour when they crucified him. And the inscription of the charge against him read, 'The King of the Jews.'"

In that moment, it appears Jesus has lost. Death lingers nearby, and it's only a matter of hours before asphyxiation takes its toll. Roman soldiers crassly gamble for his clothes as the day passes. The religious officials, Pharisees and Sadducees, have their loudest critic on a shameful display. Rome, religion, and death appear to have won. Jesus's followers have fled, with the lone exception of John. Peter has denied Jesus three times.

Suffering and Glory—The Cross, the Resurrection, and Victory

This isn't plan B. God isn't panicked in heaven, crying out, "What are we going to do?" God has only one plan, and in this moment of crisis, he's carrying it out (see Acts 2:23). Something beyond our comprehension went on within the Trinity, as the Son of God, the second member of the Trinity, breathed his last. God punished God. God's wrath was poured out in all its fullness upon God. God suffered. God was forsaken. And somehow through it, God triumphed.

> Jesus uttered a loud cry and breathed his last. And the curtain of the temple was torn in two, from top to bottom. And when the centurion, who stood facing him, saw that in this way he breathed his last, he said, "Truly this man was the Son of God!" (Mark 15:37–39)

It's no small irony that one of the Roman executioners would make this confession at this moment. It's the moment when the tide of history turns. The centurion's confession is the first hint that no government, no authority, no ruler is going to overcome the power of the cross. They can bring whatever power to bear against it, but it will only grow stronger. In fact, history shows us that the persecution of the church has only worked to spread the gospel into the pockets and corners of the world.

Theologian Peter Bolt writes that, "[Jesus's] death was the last necessary event before the coming of the kingdom, a ransom for many. The great exchange that will ransom human beings from the grave is impossible for a human being, even a rich human being, to pay. But God has done the impossible. He has supplied the ransom: eternal life in the kingdom of God is opened up by the death of the servant who gave his life as a ransom for many."[9]

The torn curtain means the end of religion. The curtain separated the world from the presence of God, and only a priest could enter the Holy of Holies behind the curtain, offer sacrifices, and provide for the forgiveness of God's people. Now, there is no system of behavior that brings one into the presence of God. There is no hierarchy of persons that can provide or prohibit access to God or his grace. There is instead only Jesus, who through the cross has become our priest, sacrifice, and tabernacle.

The religious leaders who killed Jesus are defeated. His Roman executioners are awestruck. Next up, Jesus takes on death.

On the morning of the third day, Mary Magdalene and Mary the mother of Jesus go to his tomb to anoint his body. They expect to find it, and are anxious about how they might roll away the stone that covers his tomb.

> And looking up, they saw that the stone had been rolled back—it was very large. And entering the tomb, they saw a young man sitting on the right side, dressed in a white robe, and they were alarmed. And he said to them, "Do not be alarmed. You seek Jesus of Nazareth, who was crucified. He has risen; he is not here." (Mark 16:4–6)

It's this moment that allows the apostle Paul to cry out, years later,

> "Death is swallowed up in victory."
> "O death, where is your victory?
>   O death, where is your sting?" (1 Cor. 15:54–55)

The empty tomb shows that the greatest oppression of all—the oppression of sin and death—has been defeated. It's gospel Judo. In Judo, you learn to use the power and movement of your attacker against them, often in moves that end with your opponent landing headfirst. Jesus takes on all that is plagued—he becomes human, taking upon himself all the wrath of God against sin and all the attack and oppression of death, turning it on its head to provide life for God's children.

Why did Christianity arise, and why did it take the shape it did? The early Christians themselves reply: We exist because of Jesus's resurrection.[10] Were there no resurrection, we would have neither comfort nor hope, and everything else Christ did and suffered would be in vain.[11]

The Gospel of the Cross

It's in the light of the resurrection that Peter, who always jockeyed for power amongst the disciples and who denied Jesus when the time came for him to suffer, becomes the rock, upon whom God can build a church. It's in the light of the resurrection that Peter takes on a fierce boldness in the book of Acts and can ultimately face his own execution for the sake of the gospel.

In his own epistle, he describes the gospel of the cross like this: "For Christ also suffered once for sins, the righteous for the unrighteous, that he might bring us to God, being put to death in the flesh but made alive in the spirit" (1 Pet. 3:18). In this short verse, Peter summarizes the meaning of the cross by pointing to Jesus's sacrifice, righteousness, and work of reconciliation. In what follows here, we will unpack some of the rich implications of Jesus's life, death, and resurrection through those lenses. It may require some new words, but as missiologist Ed Stetzer has said, if Christians can learn to order at Starbucks, they can probably learn to handle some theological language.[12] As we go along, we'll enlist the help of rapper Shai Linne, whose definitions are both helpful and very memorable.

Sacrifice

We'll start with the phrase, "Christ also suffered once for sins." By suffering for sins, he becomes our sacrifice. In Genesis, when Adam and Eve sinned, God covered them by taking the life of an animal, taking its skin, and clothing them. Their crimes warranted death, but God spared them by allowing a substitute to die in their place. So it was with Israel, when God established his covenant with them and a means of forgiveness through an elaborate system of sacrifices and offerings. In Hebrews 10, the author tells us that all of this is "but a shadow" (v. 1) of what Christ would accomplish on the cross. Where those sacrifices had to be offered continually (v. 1) and couldn't actually take away sin (v. 4), Jesus's sacrifice is once-and-for-all (v. 10) and is entirely effective (v. 14).

Two words that describe this are "propitiation" and "expiation." Propitiation means the judgment for our sins was fully satisfied, and expiation means our sins were actually taken away. Theologian Robert Peterson has a nice way of defining propitiation: "Propitiation is the turning away of God's wrath and expiation is the putting away of sin."[13]

Hip-hop artist Shai Linne describes it this way:

> Expiation—Expiation means God's removed my filthiness
> The Old Testament type was the goat into the wilderness . . .
> Propitiation—Propitiation means since the Lamb has died
> His work is finished—God's wrath is satisfied[14]

On the Day of Atonement, in Israel, there was a scapegoat. The priest would lay hands on the goat and declare that all of Israel's sins were put upon the goat. Then, rather than kill the goat, they would drive it off into the wilderness. It was an act of removal of guilt, separation of the sin from the redeemed people.

So redemption at the cross means that Jesus's blood is enough to pay for my sins and take them away.

Righteousness

Next, Peter says, "the righteous for the unrighteous" (1 Pet. 3:18). The cross is only properly understood when we see it as something we deserve. It requires us to acknowledge our place in the camp of the unrighteous. Paul says:

> For while we were still weak, at the right time Christ died for the ungodly. For one will scarcely die for a righteous person—though perhaps for a good person one would dare even to die—but God shows his love for us in that while we were still sinners, Christ died for us. (Rom. 5:6–8)

In doing this, a miraculous exchange takes place. Paul describes it in 2 Corinthians when he says, "For our sake he made him to be sin who knew no sin, so that in him we might become the righteousness of God" (5:18). Suddenly the unrighteousness of our lives is exchanged with Jesus's own perfect righteousness. It's what Augustus Toplady famously called the "double cure"—that we are cleansed from wrath and made pure.[15] It is both justification—we are cleansed from wrath—and imputation—credited with Jesus's own righteousness. Or as Shai Linne has said:

> Justification—God declares us righteous
> Imputation? God takes Jesus' righteousness amount
> Through faith He credits it into the Christian's account[16]

Imagine being diagnosed with terminal cancer. Over months you'll experience the toll of both the disease and the attempts to cure it: losing hair, gaining and losing weight, shedding skin, and losing all sense of comfort. Imagine now that someone comes to your hospital bed, connects himself to you with a series of tubes and cables, and suddenly begins to take on your disease. As your wounds heal, his are opened. As color and health return to your skin, they're lost from his. Eventually you're perfectly healed, and he lies there as sick as you once were. Now imagine that you've not only been healed of your disease, you'll now live forever. That's the power of the double cure. Not only are we made right with God, we're actually made righteous forever before God.

This should transform everything for us. Where in the past we were unable to please God, hindered by our sins, the cross allows us to be credited with Christ's righteousness—we're made right with God. It's as if everything I do is a gift to God through Jesus Christ. That should transform our motivations and actions dramatically. We're free from having to prove ourselves or earn approval. As Harold Best has said, we offer and Christ perfects.[17] His righteousness—his approval before God—is wonderfully given to us because of the cross.

Reconciliation

Peter's final phrase is: "that he might bring us to God." One of the promises that had echoed through history concerned God's dwelling place. When God establishes the covenant at Sinai, the end goal is to have his dwelling place with his people. Building the temple in Jerusalem was a sign to the world that God lived with Israel. Even so, a deeper promise rumbled in the background. Jeremiah tells of a day when:

> I will put my law within them, and I will write it on their hearts. And I will be their God, and they shall be my people. And no longer

shall each one teach his neighbor and each his brother, saying, "Know the LORD," for they shall all know me, from the least of them to the greatest, declares the LORD. For I will forgive their iniquity, and I will remember their sin no more. (Jer. 31:33–34)

Remember that for Jeremiah's hearers, God's presence was a deadly and dangerous thing. God told Moses, "You cannot see my face, for man shall not see me and live" (Ex. 33:20). The whole architecture of the tabernacle and temple was meant to protect men from God's presence. God's presence is a blazing holiness, and it's lethal to sinful men and women like you and me.

It's our tendency to think of the temple, with its walls and curtains, as a structure meant to keep out the riffraff. In fact, the architecture of the temple were evidence of God's grace. That distance and separation was meant to protect people from a power and glory that would destroy them. God's promise to dwell with his people, particularly to dwell in their hearts and covenant with all of them (without human mediators) must have sounded radical and frightening.

When the temple curtain tore as Jesus breathed his last, it meant that access to God's presence was opened wide. No longer did we need a priest or an intercessor; Jesus himself is our intercessor, and he's flung wide the gates to God's presence:

Therefore, brothers, since we have confidence to enter the holy places by the blood of Jesus, by the new and living way that he opened for us through the curtain, that is, through his flesh, and since we have a great priest over the house of God, let us draw near with a true heart in full assurance of faith, with our hearts sprinkled clean from an evil conscience and our bodies washed with pure water. (Heb. 10:19–22)

It's a message of reconciliation, whereby the cross has ended any division between us and God: "All this is from God, who through Christ reconciled us to himself and gave us the ministry of reconciliation" (2 Cor. 5:18). Jesus tells his followers: "No longer do I call you servants, for the servant does not know what his master is doing; but I have called you friends" (John 15:15). Because of the cross, we can now boldly encounter the presence of God, knowing that he welcomes us as friends and family. All the hostility and tension between sinners and a holy God cease. To quote Shai Linne again:

> Reconciliation means there's no more enmity
> God is now a friend to me, we're no longer enemies[18]

But the good news doesn't stop with reconciliation. Even more radically it tells us that we're mysteriously and powerfully united to Christ. This union is described both as our being in Christ and Christ's being in us. A few examples:

> So that Christ may dwell in your hearts through faith. (Eph. 3:17)

> I have been crucified with Christ. It is no longer I who live, but Christ who lives in me. And the life I now live in the flesh I live by faith in the Son of God, who loved me and gave himself for me. (Gal. 2:20)

> But he who is joined to the Lord becomes one spirit with him. (1 Cor. 6:17)

> That they may all be one, just as you, Father, are in me, and I in you, that they also may be in us, so that the world may believe that you have sent me. (John 17:21)

How exactly does this operate? What exactly does it mean that we're united with Christ? To quote John Calvin on the issue: "I rather humbly admire, than labor to comprehend this mystery. But this I confess, that by the divine power of the Spirit, life is poured from heaven upon the earth. . . . It is the work of the Spirit, that Christ dwells in us, supports and nourishes us, and performs all the functions of a head."[19]

Union with Christ is a beautiful mystery, meant to bring us comfort and strength. As Paul says, "For you have died, and your life is hidden with Christ in God" (Col. 3:3). The life-giving power of God, which raised Jesus from the dead, now dwells in you. The strength of God that endured suffering on this earth and at the cross, now is your strength. It means that you're never alone, never without the presence and power of God himself.

The Importance of the Cross

The cross is not peripheral. It's not something that we encounter at the beginning of our Christian journey and move beyond as we mature in discipleship. It's the center of our faith, the hub from which every good thing flows.

In the book of Exodus, the people of Israel were told to paint the blood of a sacrifice over their doorway, and we too live in the shadow of the blood of the Lamb. Life as a Christian is life in the comforting shadow of the cross. We're marked by Christ's blood, free from wrath and sin, and welcomed and accepted by God our Father.

Just as some want to diminish the cross by marginalizing it or ignoring it altogether, others want to treat it as a once-in-a-lifetime encounter. You become a Christian when you encounter the cross, and then you move on. The rest of your life is "discipleship." The cross has accomplished its purpose, and now you're done with it.

What a sad misunderstanding of the life-altering glory of the cross. Far from a singular experience, the cross is a center, a place we return to again and again. Each of the terms explored above is a source of hope, and it's good news we need to hear continually as we live out our lives. Consider how the cross speaks to our regular, everyday needs:

1. Do you ever feel like your sins are unforgiven? Do you ever feel like there's something you need to do to earn God's approval? Do you ever think, "If I can just get _____ taken care of (my finances, my addiction, my anger, my pride, etc.), then I'll be able to rest before God"? In such moments, you need to remind yourself that God's work is finished (propitiation). God is entirely and perfectly satisfied with the pure and sinless life of Jesus and the sacrifice of his death on your behalf. That payment is enough. Your attempts at pleasing God are like fig leaves. They won't add up, and glory to God—they don't have to!

2. Have you ever felt dirty and stained by your sins? Has it ever been hard to look at yourself in the mirror because of shame over what

you've done? Remember the goat (expiation). Your filthiness, your stains, your blemishes are all loaded on Christ and removed from you as far as the east is from the west.

3. When you wake up feeling burdened by God's anger, fearful of wrath and judgment, painfully unable to please him, you need to remember the double cure: You're safe from wrath (justification) and made pure (imputation). It means that whatever the mess of your life may be, if your faith is in Christ, you can offer your life, and Christ perfects it. Not only is God not angry with you—he delights in you.

4. And finally, when you struggle with loneliness, when you struggle with a sense that no one is by your side or understands your battles, remember that you've been reconciled to God, and moreover, he lives in you and you in him. All the resources of his strength, character, and grace are available to you in Christ Jesus. You're never alone.

Far from abstract, superfluous "head knowledge," the cross and the doctrines attached to it are at the center of worship in this life because our sin-plagued souls and sin-plagued world find their ultimate comfort and hope in them. Not only that, but the cross remains at the center of worship in the next world because it's what made that new reality possible:

> Then the angel showed me the river of the water of life, bright as crystal, flowing from the throne of God and of the Lamb through the middle of the street of the city; also, on either side of the river, the tree of life with its twelve kinds of fruit, yielding its fruit each month. The leaves of the tree were for the healing of the nations. No longer will there be anything accursed, but the throne of God and of the Lamb will be in it, and his servants will worship him. They will see his face, and his name will be on their foreheads. And night will be no more. They will need no light of lamp or sun, for the Lord God will be their light, and they will reign forever and ever. (Rev. 22:1–5)

The Bible uses many words to describe our Savior, but when it opens the curtain to eternity and allows a peek at the world to come, we see the sacrificial Lamb, whose blood covers our doorways in faith. The Savior, who died a sacrificial death on the cross, in our place, is worshiped forevermore.

Map It

Q: What is the gospel of the cross?

A: It is the good news that through faith in Jesus's perfect life, death for our sins, and victorious resurrection from the dead, we are justified and reconciled to God.

Zoom Out

The whole storyline of the Bible is haunted by images of the cross. It's promised as early as Genesis 3:15, foreshadowed in the lamb in Exodus, symbolized in the sacrificial system, and seen in the visions of the prophets. It's the turning point in the Scriptures, and it is unapologetically the center point of the entire New Testament.

Zoom In

Meditate on the stages of Jesus's life as he journeys to the cross, resurrection, and ascension.

- Incarnation—Luke 1:35; John 1:1–18; Romans 9:5; Philippians 2:5–11; Titus 2:11–13
- Sinless life—John 8:29; 15:10; 18:38; 2 Corinthians 5:21; Hebrews 4:15; 7:26; 1 Peter 1:19; 2:22; 1 John 3:5
- Death for our sins—John 3:16; Romans 3:23–25; 5:6–9; 2 Corinthians 5:21; Ephesians 2:1–10; Hebrews 2:17; 1 Peter 3:18
- Resurrection—John 20; 1 Corinthians 15:12–20; Philippians 3:8–11; Hebrews 6:1–2; 1 Peter 1:3
- Ascension—Psalm 68:18; Luke 24:50–53; John 7:33; 14:28; 16:5; Acts 1:3–9; Hebrews 10:12–13
- Exaltation—John 17:5; Acts 2:33; Philippians 2:9; 1 Timothy 3:16; Hebrews 1:3–4; Revelation 5:12
- Return—Matthew 24:44; John 14:3; Acts 1:11; Philippians 3:20; 1 Thessalonians 4:16; Titus 2:12–13; Revelation 22:20

Pray It: Ephesians 1:15–23

For this reason, because I have heard of your faith in the Lord Jesus and your love toward all the saints, I do not cease to give thanks for you, remembering you in my prayers, that the God of our Lord Jesus Christ, the Father of glory, may give you the Spirit of wisdom and of revelation in the knowledge of him, having the eyes of your hearts enlightened, that you may know what is the hope to which he has called you, what are the riches of his glorious inheritance in the saints, and what is the immeasurable greatness of his power toward us who believe, according to the working of his great might that he worked in Christ when he raised him from the dead and seated him at his right hand in the heavenly places, far above all rule and authority and power and dominion, and above every name that is named, not only in this age but also in the one to come. And he put all things under his feet and gave him as head over all things to the church, which is his body, the fullness of him who fills all in all.

3

The Gospel of Grace

My father was very sure about certain matters pertaining to the universe.
To him all good things—trout as well as eternal salvation—come by
grace and grace comes by art and art does not come easy.

NORMAN MACLEAN

American audiences have a deep love for tales of revenge. Almost every year, there's another movie or TV show in the national spotlight that is, at heart, a revenge story: Mel Gibson's *Payback*, Robert Ludlum's *The Bourne Supremacy*, Quentin Tarantino's *Kill Bill*, NBC's *Vengeance*, and many classics like *True Grit* and *The Godfather*. The list could fill the rest of this book.

At our core, we love revenge stories because of a twisted hunger for justice. In any good revenge story (like most of the ones above), there's a horrendous crime at the start of the story. *Taken*, a particularly violent tale of revenge and rescue, begins with the kidnapping of a young girl by men who traffic women for the sex trade. The horrific circumstances of the kidnapping lead the audience to cheer on as the girl's father goes on a rampage to bring her home.

These stories begin with a crime, enabling us to cheer on the protagonists as they pursue vigilante justice—hunting down the criminals and punishing anyone who stands in their way. We love these stories because we're wired to. God has given us an innate sense of justice, an inner compass that knows that crime must be punished and wrong must be righted. When injustice occurs, when crime goes unpunished or the innocent suffer, we want to know that someone is going to make it right.

The Whole Gospel

But the gospel, properly understood, disrupts our sense of justice in two ways. First, in relation to ourselves, it tells us that we're the unpunished criminal, and our crimes deserve death. The rift created by sin is unfathomably wide, and nothing we do can bridge the gap; we can't pay for our crimes and restore things to how they're meant to be. Second, God's own actions defy the logic of any good revenge story.

Imagine it: The story opens with God's goodness pouring out into creation. He creates a beautiful world, a perfect order and harmony, and in short order, it's assaulted by a band of criminals. They storm in, killing, destroying, and leaving behind a burning wasteland. Frankly, it would be a great opening to a revenge story. Something beautiful is wastefully, callously destroyed. Our hero sets out on a journey to get justice, furiously chasing down the criminals, but when he finds them, the story takes an unexpected turn. He doesn't strike them down. He doesn't punish them. Instead, he embraces them. He adopts them, telling them, "It's okay. I punished my son for what you did."

That movie would bomb. The ending makes no sense at all.

Yet this is the story of God's radical, scandalous grace. God has taken a bunch of criminals and made them his children, allowing his Son to suffer the consequences of their crimes. It defies our sense of justice. On the one hand, Jesus died innocent of any crime, and on the other, it gives us nothing to do, nothing to point to in our story by which we can claim that we've achieved something. Instead, God shows up at our hideout, breaks down the front door, and tells us that it's finished. He's taken care of everything, and we're forgiven.

We could define or describe this aspect of the gospel in many ways, but for a variety of reasons, we've chosen to use the shorthand of "grace." The gospel of God's grace is the wonderful news that God accepts us and shares his life with us not because we have earned or deserved it but because he gives it to us freely at Christ's expense.

Understood biblically, grace is nothing less than a scandal, and it's a message that insults and offends the consciences of religious people of all stripes. At the heart of religion is a belief that, properly performed, religion makes us acceptable before the eyes of God. Grace shatters that idea. It says we can never perform up to God's standards, but in Jesus, God has miraculously loved and accepted us anyway.

Grace on Display

It's a profound stumbling block, because we hate to hear the first part of that message, but it was a consistent message Jesus preached as he confronted self-righteous and religious people:

> He went out again beside the sea, and all the crowd was coming to him, and he was teaching them. And as he passed by, he saw Levi the son of Alphaeus sitting at the tax booth, and he said to him, "Follow me." And he rose and followed him. And as he reclined at table in his house, many tax collectors and sinners were reclining with Jesus and his disciples, for there were many who followed him. And the scribes of the Pharisees, when they saw that he was eating with sinners and tax collectors, said to his disciples, "Why does he eat with tax collectors and sinners?" And when Jesus heard it, he said to them, "Those who are well have no need of a physician, but those who are sick. I came not to call the righteous, but sinners." (Mark 2:13–17)

What Jesus does here is shocking. First, we need to understand what a first-century tax collector did. There's no doubt that the IRS has a way of sending chills up the spines of most Americans today, but with the IRS, you have a system that, while bureaucratic and fearsome, is perfectly legal and fair. As citizens, we have a responsibility to pay our taxes, and the IRS is only making sure we keep up our end of the deal.

Not so with Roman tax collectors. Far from a cold bureaucracy enforced by accountants and lawyers, the Roman system was randomly enforced by low-level thugs. Their first job was to make sure that the Romans got their fair share from everyone. Their second job was to enrich themselves. If you owed $200 to the Romans, the collector could take $500 and pocket the difference. It didn't matter to the Romans. To make things worse, Levi was a Jew. His work for the Romans was a betrayal to his Jewish brethren, taking their money and sending it off to their oppressors.

Yet here we see Jesus, God of Israel in human flesh, befriending

The Whole Gospel

Levi. Of all the folks in the crowds, of all the devoted religious leaders to whom he could've reached out, Jesus, instead, calls out Levi: betrayer of his brothers and sisters, cheating, money-grubbing Levi.

This isn't a fluke or an accident. Jesus is intentionally communicating something to all who are watching. It's called "grace." Unmerited favor. Love unlooked for, unexpected, and undeserved. As pastor and theologian Paul Zahl puts it, "Grace is love that seeks you out when you have nothing to give in return. Grace is love coming at you that has nothing to do with you. Grace is being loved when you are unlovable. It's being loved when you are the opposite of lovable.[1]

Rather than being the exception, the calling of Levi is the rule. Jesus further illustrates his point at Levi's house, when he's surrounded by tax collectors and sinners. He's surrounded by outsiders but he isn't rebuking and berating them. He's partying with them. Sharing a meal in Jesus's time meant far more than it does now.[2] In Luke's account of the same story, it's referred to as a banquet, a celebratory feast that would have lasted for hours, an act of communion and solidarity. Jesus comes to sinners and welcomes them as family, giving them a sense of belonging and solidarity with the God of the universe.

The Offense of Grace

The religious crowd was furious. Jesus was clearly someone with power and authority from God, and yet his presence amongst these sinners defied everything they believed about how to live and please God. Such company was unclean, unfit, and unwelcome at worship. For the Pharisees, you ate, bathed, dressed, and went about your business with great care, so as not to make yourself "unclean." Jesus, a respected religious teacher, flagrantly ignores all of those barriers, dining with the most "unclean" members of society. "Why?" the leaders ask. Jesus's response is, "Those who are well have no need of a physician, but those who are sick. I came not to call the righteous, but sinners" (Mark 2:17).

It turns the world of the Pharisees upside down. Their whole lives were dedicated to purifying themselves and making themselves acceptable to God. But God shows up and says that those efforts are both ineffective and (perhaps most infuriating) unnecessary.

Grace offends because it exposes. It exposes our sins, showing that we've underestimated the depths of our problem, and it exposes our helplessness; God doesn't need any help from us for the cure.

Not long ago, the actor Charlie Sheen had a very public meltdown. The press revealed a combination of drug use, allegations of parental negligence, and bitter feuding with studio executives, and the world watched with mouths agape as Sheen gave interview after interview, his words becoming more bizarre, his perspective more twisted. "What are you doing?" someone asked him. "Winning," he said, blind to his own downward spiral.

So it was with the scribes and Pharisees. Jesus knew that their souls were tortured and sin-sick, but their lives put up a shiny, white-washed appearance of having it all together. "Duh, winning." They were oblivious to the depths of their problem.

If we lack a sufficient awareness of the depths of our sins, then we'll underestimate how great a cure is needed to heal them. The prophet Jeremiah laments: "The heart is deceitful above all things, and desperately sick; who can understand it?" (Jer. 17:9). The author of Ecclesiastes agrees, saying: "Also, the hearts of the children of man are full of evil, and madness is in their hearts while they live, and after that they go to the dead" (Eccles. 9:3).

And yet, in spite of this situation, grace boldly declares that our desperate state is no longer a hindrance between God and us. As Paul said, "There is therefore now no condemnation for those who are in Christ Jesus" (Rom. 8:1). This isn't because we've cleaned ourselves and made ourselves presentable; it's because he's single-handedly made a way to accept us, mess and all. God joins sinners for a feast, and it shames the self-righteous religious elites. Jesus wouldn't be found among the talking heads that seek to diagnose and condemn celebrities who are having public meltdowns. He'd be found at dinner with Charlie Sheen.

The Whole Gospel

The Enemies of Grace

This brings us to the two great enemies of grace, two monsters that lurk in our hearts and keep us from wholeheartedly embracing this radical aspect of the gospel: entitlement and performance. They blind us to the desperate need and hopeless situation that only grace can cure.

Entitlement: The First Enemy of Grace

While certainly nothing new, the disease of entitlement has risen to new heights in our contemporary culture. Its evil twin is narcissism, "an inordinate preoccupation with the self," the self-obsession that has begun running rampant in our self-absorbed, social-media–saturated culture.[3]

The mythical Greek character Narcissus died when he fell in love with his own image. He was so captivated by his reflection in a pool of water that he fell in and drowned. Hence narcissism is not merely self-worth, but self-worship, and the myth shows us its disastrous consequences.

Narcissism plagues North America today. Our self-admiration begins with the messages we hear in childhood: "You're a princess" or "You're a rock star." In elementary school, we are told over and over that we can do anything when we grow up—dream big. Of course, this is simply untrue. Most of us could never be an astronaut or a professional athlete or a supermodel. We can't become "anything," but a self-esteem culture insists we must delude children into denying any sense of limits. Seemingly harmless streams of encouragement create a generation obsessed with itself, obsessed with image and fame, believing deeply that they're "special" and "unique." David Brooks recently said, "We're an overconfident species. . . . American students no longer perform particularly well in global math tests. But Americans are among the world leaders when it comes to thinking that we are really good at math."[4] We are enraptured with our own reflections.

It's tempting to believe that the self-obsessed and self-congratulatory behavior we see on places like Facebook and Twitter are actually cover-ups for insecurity, masking a generation that is deeply uncomfortable with themselves. Jean Twenge and Keith Campbell, in their excellent book *The Narcissism Epidemic*, say it's quite the opposite: "It turns out that deep down, narcissists think they're awesome."[5]

This pervasive attitude doesn't stop at our church doors. Campbell and Twenge tell us, "Originally, religions could enforce narcissism-reducing practices because they didn't have to compete for adherents: if you were born into a religion, you usually stayed. Now, however, people can select the religion that works for them—often the one that offers the most benefits with the least pain. To compete, religions have to give people what they want. Because reducing narcissism is not always pleasant, most people are not going to attend churches that demand humility."[6]

They cite Joel Osteen, pastor of Lakewood Church and best-selling author of *Your Best Life Now* and *Every Day a Friday*, as one of the more prominent and glaring purveyors of religious narcissism. "God didn't create you to be average," Osteen writes (leaving unanswered the pertinent question: if God doesn't want anyone to be average, doesn't that change the average?), "You were made to excel."[7] Catering to the self-admiration of our culture leads to a kind of spiritual exceptionalism. "God must love me because I'm so loveable." Narcissists genuinely believe that they're wonderful, and they gravitate toward messages that affirm their belief.

It's a stunning and painful blast for narcissists to be confronted with the Jesus of the Bible, who refuses the company of the "above average" and the "excellent," choosing instead to associate with the corrupt and the broken. Jesus's decision to take company with the sick rather than the healthy exposes the so-called healthy one's disease. For the scribes, their objection to Jesus's feast with Levi and his friends would have begun with their own status as exceptional, holy, and separate people; they believed they were entitled to the presence of God. The gospel of grace is a message that can be heard only by those who are aware of their own brokenness and need. It's a message that's exceedingly difficult to hear in a culture that tells us that we deserve everything: happiness, low interest rates, affordable health care, a skinny body, and a fat wallet. The gospel of grace insists that we deserve none of this, and points to the anguish of God nailed to the cross as the proper measure of what we deserve. Without such a signpost, there's nothing amazing about grace.

Performance: The Second Enemy of Grace

The second enemy of grace is performance. This would have been the scribes' second appeal. Even if the whole world was a sinful mess, at least they had obeyed the rules and done what they could to cleanse themselves. "Doesn't obedience mean that God owes us something in return?"

Where entitlement begins with the belief that we're inherently wonderful, performance acknowledges (to varying degrees) that we're sinful, and it prescribes religious behavior for the cure. If we can just get our behavior right, we can once again be acceptable to God.

If entitlement's evil twin is narcissism, performance's evil twin is religion. Religion declares that if we behave properly, we belong to God. It's aware of our guilt and appeals to adherence to a set of moralistic standards (I'm good enough), religious habits (I'm spiritual enough), or spiritual knowledge (I'm smart enough) to justify us before God.[8] These behaviors become the way we deal with our guilty consciences. If we keep up our end of the bargain, God owes us a ticket to heaven, and perhaps a good life today, too.

I'm Good Enough.

Moralism—the idea that "I'm good enough"—is wrapped up and packaged neatly in our churches today. Whenever Christianity is defined in terms of behavior (dos and don'ts), it's knocking on the door of moralism. It understands the cross to be a way in which Jesus gave us a fresh start, leaving it up to us to get it right from now on. "You've certainly got a fresh start," moralism says, "but don't screw it up now." Moralistic Christianity requires living up to these standards, being ready to tell Jesus "I'm good enough—I kept up my end of the bargain" when we get to heaven's gates.

In practice, though, moralism is brutal. We perpetually run up against our sinful flesh, and our best efforts result only in deepening frustrations. We end up one of three ways: deceiving ourselves into thinking that we don't struggle with sin, excusing ourselves and making up justifications for the sins we do see, or despairing of ourselves, realizing we can't win the war with our own flesh.

I'm Spiritual Enough.
Some religion puts its confidence in religious activity. Its confidence isn't in the work of Jesus, but in the work of a priest, intercessor, or ritual. Protestants are quick to criticize Roman Catholicism, which sees the sacraments (baptism, the Eucharist, prayers, penances, etc.) as actual cleansing work, but don't think for a moment that we Protestants aren't quick to get in on the action. For instance, there's a lot of conscience-absolving that happens around the daily "quiet time."

"If I can just read my Bible and pray more, my life will go better, God will be pleased with me, and my conscience won't feel so weighty." If you ask Christians how their spiritual life is going, you often get an accounting of their quiet times—how regular, how long, etc. It's the gauge by which many measure their spiritual health.

Worship too becomes a salve for guilty consciences. We treat our worship leaders as priests, expecting them to lead us into God's presence in a way that is inaccessible apart from their charisma, emotion, and music. Every time we credit a worship leader with "leading us into God's presence," we are anointing them as priests, and crediting them with doing something that only Jesus can do.[9]

This "I'm spiritual enough" religiosity is all about experience. It can be traditional or contemporary, charismatic or cessationist, but it always depends on a sense of spiritual experience or religious action to make us right with God. Robert Capon describes this way of thinking as "plain, ordinary, religion-type religion":

> Burning incense at the evening sacrifice, pouring chicken blood on the sacred stone at sunrise, standing on your head and praying all night with your right thumb stuck in your left ear, trying with

might, main, and promises of reform to expiate your irremovable guilt. What's that all about? Why do we all do it? Well, to be honest, we do it to fake out a repair job on the hopelessly messed-up inside of our heads, to kid ourselves into the impression that there is still something we can do—in short, to avoid facing the fact that we are dead and only grace can raise us.[10]

I'm Smart Enough.

Knowledge itself—of the Scriptures and theology—is yet another conscience-cleanser. This "I'm smart enough" religiosity relies on having all the right answers as the key for confidence in salvation. Such a person has a shelf full of books, answers to every catechism question, and a readiness to fight anyone that crosses him. In fact, the great virtue of the religion of spiritual knowledge is contentiousness, a readiness to pick a fight and defend the doctrine that has saved us.

But the book of James reminds us that even demons have sound doctrine (James 2:19), and it does them no good. We should take no comfort in having the right answers—they merely point to a Savior who actually accomplished the only thing that can comfort guilty souls; they do nothing to cure what ails us.

Performance and Entitlement Never Add Up to Enough

None of us is good enough, spiritual enough, or smart enough. The prophet Isaiah tells us:

> We have all become like one who is unclean,
>   and all our righteous deeds are like a polluted garment.
> We all fade like a leaf,
>   and our iniquities, like the wind, take us away. (Isa. 64:6)

If we underestimate the depths of our sin, we will underestimate the cure. You don't bring a squirt gun to a bazooka fight, as they say, and we don't fight Satan, sin, and death with a Bible study, a worship song, a clean voting record, or a tithe check. Only something so dramatic as a holy God suffering and dying in our place can provide a cure.

The church has always struggled with this. In Acts 15, the church was wrestling with the inclusion of Gentiles (bringing in religious outsiders), and Peter affirmed, "We believe that we will be saved through the grace of the Lord Jesus, just as they will" (v. 11). Belonging to Christ, he says, has nothing to do with the proper pedigree. Paul affirms this from a different perspective when he says that not all who descended from "Israel belong to Israel" (Rom. 9:6). Instead of relying on genealogy and religious culture, being one of God's people is a matter of faith in the work of the one true Son of God. Religious-earning and man-made righteousness are now thrown in the trash heap like old, worn-out appliances. They do us no good. Paul says:

> What shall we say, then? That Gentiles who did not pursue righteousness have attained it, that is, a righteousness that is by faith; but that Israel who pursued a law that would lead to righteousness did not succeed in reaching that law. (Rom. 9:30–31)

What a strange new world . . . Israel is condemned for trying to make themselves acceptable, and Gentiles are accepted for trusting in the acceptability of another.

When the Galatian church is led astray and comes to believe that the cross also requires the rite of circumcision to save, Paul furiously rebukes them:

> O foolish Galatians! Who has bewitched you? It was before your eyes that Jesus Christ was publicly portrayed as crucified. Let me ask you only this: Did you receive the Spirit by works of the law or by hearing with faith? Are you so foolish? Having begun by the Spirit, are you now being perfected by the flesh? (Gal. 3:1–3)

The same rebuke could be levied against any religious observance. We should take no comfort from our good works, no comfort from our good thinking, and no comfort from our ceremonial faithfulness—even if that faithfulness is to the evangelical-approved rites of quiet times, worship services, and faithful tithing. You'll never be smart enough, good enough, or spiritual enough to please God. None of these can heal our sickness, and none of them can distinguish us from a godless world. All of us are just like the broken, sick, money-grubbing outsiders that Jesus gathers with in Mark 2. Refusal to acknowledge that fact places us amongst the scribes and Pharisees.

The gospel declares that our right standing with God and our continued life in his kingdom are *all* a gift of his grace. Life with God comes by grace. The cross is given to us by grace. We have life with God not because of anything we have or could have done or anything we have failed to do but because God has freely given it to us at Jesus's expense. We are safe, we are accepted, we are loved because God has made it so by his grace. Period.

Imagine an explorer embarking on a journey into unknown lands. There are rumors of rough seas and fierce savages in these unknown lands. His life is in peril, as are the lives of his men. Imagine, then, if just after he sets sail, an angel appears and gives him a map that promises safe passage. It details the safest path across the sea, the safe path through rocks on the shore of the new land, and the places where natives are likely to be hospitable. Suddenly, a journey that should have been deadly is now as safe and secure as a walk in the park. That's the map of grace. It shows us that we're safe, welcome, and that all the perils have been traversed by Jesus, who pioneered our way to enter life with God.

Knowing how prone we all are to forget this fundamental truth, Martin Luther once famously wrote, "Most necessary it is, therefore, that we should know this article well, teach it unto others, and beat it into their heads continually."[11]

A place where we see this so clearly at Sojourn is in our member interviews. In membership classes, we seek to clarify and define the gospel, and in the follow-up interviews for those who want to be members, we try to ask questions that will demonstrate how our members are putting it all together. We ask them to share their stories and the gospel, and most people do that well. Almost everyone gets tripped up, though, when we ask them how their spiritual life is going. Faces turn white, eyes drop, and they quickly say they aren't doing enough. They aren't reading their Bible enough, they aren't praying enough. It's all about their doing.

That's how most Christians define their spiritual life; it's about my performance, my ability to keep up with whatever I deem is expected of me as a cultural Christian. Rarely, when asked about their spiritual lives, do people immediately talk about God's free grace.

The reality, though, should look completely different. When people ask us how our spiritual life is doing, our reflexive answer, no matter what else is happening in our lives, should be to say that it's great, not because we've performed well, and not because our circumstances are good, or because we just advanced socially in some way, but because our life is hid with Christ in God and we are completely acceptable to the Father through his lavish, free grace.

The Grace That Saves Us Motivates Us

Few have better articulated the meaning of the gospel of grace than slave-trader-turned-pastor John Newton, author of "Amazing Grace." Newton said:

> You have one hard lesson to learn, that is, the evil of your own heart: you know something of it, but it is needful that you should know more; for the more we know of ourselves, the more we shall prize and love Jesus and His salvation. . . .
>
> Our sins are many, but his mercies are more: our sins are great, but his righteousness is greater: we are weak, but He is power. . . .
>
> Wait on the Lord, and He will enable you to see more and more of the power and grace of our High Priest. . . . This is God's way: you are not called to buy, but to beg: not to be strong in yourself, but in the grace that is in Christ Jesus.[12]

Grace levels the playing field before the eyes of God, exposing each of us before him and one another as sinners in profound need of grace. It's the failure of religion that makes grace's success amazing. It's the depths of our sins that exposes the heights of his mercy. It's our helplessness that shows us the wonder of his helpfulness.

The gospel of grace places the Christian in a strange new world where all of our sin—past, present, and future—is covered by the work of Jesus. The whole business of attempting to prove our worth in life is wiped away, and in Jesus, "There is therefore now no condemnation" (Rom. 8:1). You might object, "That sounds like we can do whatever we want." You're starting to get it. "But people will abuse this!" Now you're really getting it.

This is why grace can be such a stumbling block for Christians. First of all, most of us are strongly committed Pharisees in some corners of our hearts. We love the comfort we receive when we do our self-congratulatory religious practices. We love feeling good for doing them and seeing others as weak for failing in them. It's a power play, even if only for our private entertainment. But we also need the guardrails of religion because we're terrified to face the question, "What would we do without them?"

Paul asks the notorious question in Romans 6: "What shall we say then? Are we to continue in sin that grace may abound?" (v. 1), and we all begin to squirm in our seats. If grace means that our religion merits us nothing, then why on earth would we torture ourselves with moral purity, monogamy, and sobriety? If I can literally do nothing to save myself, then why shouldn't I commit myself to a life of doing nothing?

Such a line of questioning reveals that in our heart of hearts, we've missed out on the heart of the gospel. It's an invitation, an opportunity of extraordinary significance, and the best news we've ever heard.

God isn't holding out on us. His call to abstain from sin isn't a punishment for all that we've done wrong. We're not being chastised; we're being healed. Consider Paul's own response to his question:

> By no means! How can we who died to sin still live in it? Do you not know that all of us who have been baptized into Christ Jesus were baptized into his death? We were buried therefore with him by baptism into death, in order that, just as Christ was raised from the dead by the glory of the Father, we too might walk in newness of life. (Rom. 6:2–4)

Paul's response is not to say, "Don't do it! You'll ruin everything if you sin again!" He's saying, "You don't get it! You don't live in that world anymore. Everything has changed because of the gospel!"

It's like the difference between being a zombie and being a living person. Zombies have no interest in literature or science, no table manners, no concern for job skills and personal marketability. They're focused only on eating brains and moaning. They're dead to literature, dead to music, dead to a family meal. If they're miraculously healed, they'll suddenly be alive to all of these things. "Should we keep eating brains so that we'll be all the happier not to be zombies anymore?" By no means! You're not a zombie anymore!

Consider some of the New Testament commands. Ask yourself: Is it better to give than receive? Is it better to serve or to be served? Is it better to be a one-woman man than it is to "unite yourself with a prostitute" (1 Cor. 6:15 niv)? The grace that saves us is grace that changes us.

Moralistic religion lays these commands in front of you as hurdles to jump. "Do this, and you'll be accepted." Grace, on the other hand, lays them before you as an invitation. You were dead to all of them before, unable to do them with joy, but now, the pressure is off—the race was won by Jesus before the starting pistol fired. Instead, these commands are an invitation to a better way to live, and they come with the power of the Spirit who is bringing life to your body and soul and can help you accomplish them. Before, you were as likely to do these things in a God-pleasing way as a cow is to start doing trigonometry, but now you're part of a new creation, where sin is dying and grace is abundant.

This brings us back to the parable of buried treasure (from chap. 1). Remember that the one who's throwing aside everything he has to buy the plot of land isn't crazy. He isn't suffering for a greater good either; he isn't "suffering" at all. Every deal made at his garage sale and on eBay, every ounce of plasma given to the blood bank and every extra shift he worked is a pure joy because he knows what's coming. Such a vision of life-transforming grace is the only thing that can make us say with Paul, "For I consider that the sufferings of this present time are not worth comparing with the glory that is to be revealed to us" (Rom. 8:18).

God graciously reveals himself, befriends us, and by opening our eyes to his glory, motivates us with a hope that is powerful enough to overcome any obstacle, any cost, any pain. When we're oppressed and overwhelmed by our sin, we need to turn to the fountain of God's grace, and ask him to open our eyes. We cling to our sins because we don't believe that Jesus is better. We cling to our religion because we don't believe that grace is better. But this is blindness. We need a fresh encounter with God's grace—something only he can do in our hearts—that transforms the way we see the world. At its core, God's grace is not a principle; it's a person. We seek him—we seek Jesus, and discover the life-altering power of God's grace in his presence.

That encounter is utterly transforming. Pastor Tullian Tchividjian, in his excellent book *Surprised by Grace*, tells a story that beautifully illustrates the grace-motivated life.

> There's a story told, from Civil War days before America's slaves were freed, about a northerner who went to a slave auction and purchased a young slave girl. As they walked away from the auction, the man turned to the girl and told her, "You're free."
>
> With amazement she responded, "You mean, I'm free to do whatever I want?"
>
> "Yes," he said.
>
> "And to say whatever I want to say?"
>
> "Yes, anything."
>
> "And to be whatever I want to be?"
>
> "Yep."
>
> "And even go wherever I want to go?"
>
> "Yes," he answered with a smile. "You're free to go wherever you'd like."
>
> She looked at him intently and replied, "Then I will go with you."[13]

Whatever this transformed life is, it's certainly not a life of grueling obligation. Following Jesus, we're told, is an easy yoke and a light burden, one that proves its worth as we taste and see him. It's the greatest treasure the world has ever known, a life lived to the fullest, the way it was meant to be lived in all of its soul-satisfying wonder— grace from the first moment of our new life to the last breath we take. As Newton said in his famous hymn:

'Tis grace has brought me safe thus far,
And grace will lead me home.[14]

This is how grace works. The pressure is off. We step into a life where God has accepted us at Christ's expense, and where his power and presence transforms us. It's a radical freedom—freedom from our sins, freedom to follow Jesus.

Religion yells, "Do this, do that, keep it all together." But the gospel speaks to us and says, "Its grace, grace, grace—all grace, a gift from start to finish."

Map It

Q: What is the gospel of grace?

A: The gospel of grace is the good news of God's wonderful acceptance of us not because we have earned it or deserve it but because he gives it to us freely at Christ's expense.

Zoom Out

God's grace is evident throughout the story of the Bible. Grace shows up the moment Adam and Eve first sin, when God clothes them and shows mercy. It's evident in how he relentlessly keeps his promise to Abraham and Abraham's descendants, even as they abandon him, forget him, and turn to other gods. And of course, it's most evident in Jesus, who makes a way for sinners to be once-and-for-all restored to fellowship with God.

God's love toward his children is never contingent upon their obedience—we have nothing to earn or deserve—but is always dependent upon his promises.

Zoom In

We can see God's grace up close in a variety of ways. We see it in big ways when we see friends or family members called to Jesus. We see it in our own lives when we journey from death to life.

But we see it in small ways, too. We see it in the joy of a good meal or in a joy-filled day. We see it in God's provision for us and his protection of us. We see it in every good gift that we experience throughout our lives.

Pray It: Ephesians 3:14–21

> For this reason I bow my knees before the Father, from whom every family in heaven and on earth is named, that according to the riches of his glory he may grant you to be strengthened with power through his Spirit in your inner being, so that Christ may dwell in your hearts through faith—that you, being rooted and grounded in love, may have strength to comprehend with all the saints what is the breadth and length and height and depth, and to know the love of Christ that surpasses knowledge, that you may be filled with all the fullness of God.
>
> Now to him who is able to do far more abundantly than all that we ask or think, according to the power at work within us, to him be glory in the church and in Christ Jesus throughout all generations, forever and ever. Amen.

4

Why We Need a Whole Gospel

Watch out for people who call themselves religious;
make sure you know what they mean—make sure
they know what they mean!

JOHN IRVING

Anyone who's ever gotten into an argument with a young universalist at a coffee shop has probably heard the "elephant analogy." It's about a group of blindfolded people who are taken into a room with an elephant. They're told that God is in the middle of the room, and they're instructed to go and touch him and tell everyone what God is like.

The first man goes to the elephant and touches its side, saying, "God is big and wide, like a desert. He heaves deep breaths and his flanks move in slow rhythms."

The next goes to the elephant and touches his trunk, saying, "No, God is like a great python, long and sleek, curling and arching."

Still another, who touched the elephant's ear, says, "God is like a sail, or a wing, able to catch the wind."

And so on.

The idea of the metaphor is to say that the religions of the world are like these men, fumbling in the dark and making claims in ignorance, unable to see the whole thing. (Only the universalist, in this metaphor, lacks a blindfold.)

The best Christian response to this analogy is to point to Jesus as the answer to the confusion. Jesus leaves nothing to chance, removes our blinders, and reveals the whole picture to us. While world religions send us on a quest to find God, Jesus shows up in our world. But the metaphor itself is not without value. It's actually a pretty good way to describe the culture of hype and confusion in the church.

Some, enraptured by the message of the kingdom of God, say, "The gospel is about the kingdom." In terms of the metaphor, they're yelling. "It's all about this snakelike thing!"

Others, who are most moved by the substitutionary atonement of the cross, say, "It's a sail! It moves with the wind and flaps like a wing."

Yet others, wowed by grace, say, "It's big and wide!"[1]

Frankly, you could replace the kingdom, the cross, and grace in the analogy above with all kinds of theological ideas or methodologies. Hype and fads shout at the top of their lungs, contradicting one another and claiming to have "figured it all out." But they lack a broad and holistic perspective.

The cure here is the same as the cure above. They each cling to a map fragment and claim to have the whole thing. We need Jesus to take off our blinders. We need to see, as the Scriptures see, the gospel as a whole, beautiful, coherent unity.

It's fascinating reading to examine the way that pastors and theologians define the gospel. Trevin Wax has assembled a wide-ranging collection of definitions for the gospel at his blog, from historical figures to contemporary, from Catholic to emergent to evangelical.[2] It's particularly interesting when you begin looking for which aspect each definition emphasizes. Three examples are helpful to the conversation here.

Craig Bartholomew's definition is kingdom focused: "*Gospel* (from the Old English gōdspel, 'good tale') means 'good news,' and this is the best news there can be: in Jesus, the kingdom of God has come!"[3]

Puritan theologian Richard Sibbes defines the gospel in terms of grace, saying: "What is the gospel itself but a merciful moderation, in which Christ's obedience is esteemed ours, and our sins laid upon him, wherein God, from being a judge, becomes our Father, pardoning our sins and accepting our obedience, though feeble and blemished? We are now brought to heaven under the covenant of grace by a way of love and mercy."[4]

One of John Piper's definitions is strongly cross-focused: "The heart of the gospel is the good news that Christ died for our sins and was raised from the dead. What makes this good news is that Christ's death accomplished a perfect righteousness before God and suffered a perfect condemnation from God, both of which are counted as ours through faith alone, so that we have eternal life with God in the new heavens and the new earth."[5]

It would be tempting to assume that these men, and many others in Wax's collection, are at odds with each other, but that's not necessarily the case. Theologian John Frame, who has probably done some of the most significant work on understanding the gospel in multiple perspectives, helps to bridge the gap between the various definitions.

> Not all the differences between thinkers are differences between truth and falsity, right and wrong; factual disagreements; or differences between clear thinking and "mistakes." Some are also differences in perspective, looking at the same truth from different angles. . . . We cannot see everything at once, as God does. So we must investigate things, first from this angle, then from that.[6]

Elsewhere, Frame argues that any aspect of the gospel, properly understood, "will include true understandings of the others."[7] It's a testimony to the unity of the gospel that one can press into each of the above definitions and find one's way into the other aspects.

Dr. Piper is a great case study. In the above quote, his definition seems to have primary emphasis on the cross. In *The Passion of Jesus Christ*, his definition has more of a radical grace flavor: "The gospel of Christ is the good news that at the cost of his Son's life, God has done everything necessary to enthrall us with what will make us eternally and ever increasingly happy, namely, himself."[8]

And then in "The Gospel in 6 Minutes," he takes up the language of the kingdom of God-Jesus, the Warrior-King who has conquered all of his enemies: "The Gospel is the news that Jesus Christ, the

The Whole Gospel

Righteous One, died for our sins and rose again, eternally triumphant over all his enemies, so that there is now no condemnation for those who believe, but only everlasting joy."[9]

Dr. Piper's varied definitions are a beautiful example of how rich the gospel is. Like a jazz musician, Piper has learned the music of the gospel, and his descriptions and definitions can be freely improvised, bringing out varied nuances and exploring different angles and lenses. His definitions—like many in Wax's collection—imply the whole without necessarily saying the whole.

The great temptation is to allow one aspect to overshadow or compete with the others. Over the last three chapters, we've unpacked the gospel in three aspects—cross, kingdom, and grace. The case we're making is that the gospel is not simply a kingdom message or a cross message or a grace message—it's all three. Our tendency, for a variety of reasons, is to splinter the message, to exalt one aspect over the others, and to diminish the scope and impact of the others. By doing this, it is we who suffer, missing out on the totality of the message of the gospel. Fred Sanders describes it like this:

> When evangelicalism wanes into an anemic condition . . . it happens in this way: the points of emphasis are isolated from the main body of Christian truth and handled as if they are the whole story rather than the key points. Instead of teaching the full counsel of God (incarnation, ministry of healing and teaching, crucifixion, resurrection, ascension, and second coming), anemic evangelicalism simply shouts its one point of emphasis louder and louder (the cross! the cross! the cross!). But in isolation from the total matrix of Christian truth, the cross doesn't make the right kind of sense. A message about nothing but the cross is not emphatic. It is reductionist. The rest of the matrix matters: the death of Jesus is salvation partly because of the life he lived before it, and certainly because of the new life he lived after it, and above all because of the eternal background in which he is the eternal Son of the eternal Father. You do not need to say all of those things at all times, but you need to have a felt sense of their force behind the things you do say. When that felt sense is not present, or is not somehow communicated to the next generation, emphatic evangelicalism becomes reductionist evangelicalism.[10]

Too often, these aspects, which the Scriptures present as complementary, are pitted against one another, as though the cross were somehow an opposing message to the kingdom, or to grace. The cycle is predictable—one voice emphasizes one aspect, another responds by overreacting, emphasizing another. We divorce what God has put together, reducing the gospel and thereby weakening the power and scope of this wonderful message, and a divorced gospel is no gospel at all.

Emphasizing Only the Kingdom

For some, the gospel becomes all about the message of a new kingdom. Not unlike the disciples, there is a hunger to see the oppressive political powers that rule our world crushed and defeated. The message of God's invading kingdom is a profoundly hopeful one to people under the thumb of dictators, prejudice, and abuse.

Jesus, though, repeatedly refused attempts to install him in a temporal, political kingdom. In fact, he avoided political controversy altogether. When he was cornered on a taxation issue, Jesus turned around and paid his taxes, all the while demonstrating a power that surpassed the very political authority to which he was submitting.

Jesus wants our eyes set on a kingdom greater than an earthly one. This is a greater, far-surpassing hope than any human revolution can provide.

Reducing the gospel to be only or primarily about the kingdom of God often results in an ethic of activism, be it political or social. The gospel becomes about doing things for God, acting in the world on his behalf, fighting oppression, and raising up the downtrodden. Advancing the kingdom is the priority, and matters like doctrine are dismissed as unproductive navel-gazing. We would do best, proponents of this propose, if we were to focus on moving the mission forward, making the world a better place. This kind of Christianity means doing much for God without knowing him, without allowing him to define himself through his Word.

There is nothing wrong with the church being an agent for social, cultural, and political change in the world, but if that becomes the defining characteristic and message of the church, then we've lost sight of the deep problem that sin is in the human heart—even the heart of the religious activist. It's a problem that can only be solved by the God who died in our place, whose radical grace required nothing of us in order to be rescued.

Historically, an overemphasis on the kingdom will cause a drift toward liberalism, allowing the fact of the cross and resurrection to serve only as myth and metaphor, a symbol of resistance against the oppressors of the world. Most tragically, liberalism ends up diminishing or denying the cosmic and spiritual aspects of the gospel. Liberalism fights against visible political kingdoms, when the greater struggle is against the spiritual forces of evil that stand behind these instruments of oppression. As Kevin Spacey says in *The Usual Suspects*, "The greatest trick the Devil ever pulled was convincing the world that he didn't exist."

Emphasizing Only the Cross

Some watch that drift toward liberalism and react with a spirit of fear and protectiveness. The gospel is a pure thing, and any assault on it—particularly assaults on the importance and historicity of the cross—must be counterattacked and defended.

But overreacting leads to a weird kind of hedging. Out of a desire to protect the purity of the gospel, we tend to narrowly define it as atonement alone, and the broad pictures of God's kingdom turning back the curse and God's grace lifting up the lowly are pushed to the periphery of conversation about the gospel.

The Bible, though, seems to have no fear or reluctance about the message of God's kingdom. Jesus certainly didn't worry about overemphasizing it—and he was probably the single most misunderstood person in human history. Yet in the name of "protection," we hedge the gospel and diminish the importance of God's message about his kingdom.

Churches that emphasize only the cross often become dogmatic, making knowledge and doctrine (particularly about atonement) the most important thing in the Christian life. They might have a five-year-long sermon series on the book of Romans or require catechism memorization for membership, but though they strive to know all about God, they struggle to experience the joy of God. Church is a place where our heads are filled, though our hands tend to stay idle. You're "in" if you've got the right answers; you're "out" if you don't (or if you ask too many questions).

The message of the kingdom enriches the message of the cross by showing us that there's a whole life into which God is inviting us through the work of his Son. If these aspects are divorced, the cross can become a distant thing, a historical fact that we're thankful for, but one involving people we've never met rather than involving our neighbor down the street.

Emphasizing Only Grace

Some believers, encountering the radical message of grace in the New Testament, build their whole spirituality upon that encounter. What matters is that Jesus came to be with sinners, and though the cross isn't explicitly denied, it's often treated as an unpleasant point of history that merely shows us how much God loves us.

Churches that emphasize only grace become overly sentimental. There's a way to get addicted to the emotional experience of grace and make it the central feature of the Christian life. It motivates a certain kind of service and evangelism, but without the message of the cross to show us how desperate our need is, our service becomes more about us than others. Rather than wanting to reach out to a dying world, we're motivated by the experience of being gracious, like Jesus was. I serve others for my sake; it's my opportunity to experience yet more grace.

Aspect	Vice
Kingdom	Social Activism
Cross	Dogmatism
Grace	Sentimentalism

The Whole Gospel

Why We Need a Whole Gospel

We need an understanding of the gospel that brings clarity and unity. Whatever the cause may be—whether we're talking about business, sports, or military conquest—it's necessary to get clarity about the mission. Clarity focuses efforts and energies, defining what we are and aren't about, making the end goal clear.

The gospel isn't a message in tension with itself. It's not something that's conflicted or self-contradictory. But it's also not simplistic. If we believe that the gospel is a fundamental truth that transforms the whole world, why would we be surprised when we find that it's not easily reduced to a catch phrase or bumper sticker?

We're not saying that gospel summaries aren't true. Billy Graham's "Bridge to Life," or the "Romans Road," or the "Two Ways to Live" summaries are all true, but they each unpack only one aspect of the gospel. If one were to create similar summaries based on the gospel of the kingdom or the gospel of grace, they too would be true. Following Jesus should mean that we explore the full spectrum of gospel, with all of its depth and width.

There's an episode of *Curb Your Enthusiasm* where Larry—the show's caustic lead character—stops by the home of his friends Jeff and Susie Greene to pick up a script. They've just moved in, and Larry stands in the foyer chatting with Jeff about the script. Susie rounds the corner and is eager to show Larry around the new house, saying, "Let me give you the tour."

> Larry: Uh, you know what? It's okay, I get it.
> Susie: What do you mean?
> Larry: Ah, you know. It's bedrooms, bathrooms, I get it. I see it. It's beautiful, it's great.

Susie explodes, cursing Larry and kicking him out of the house.[11]

Often, we're just like Larry. We stand in the foyer, complimenting the window treatments and flooring, without realizing that there's more to explore. "I get it. I see it. This gospel thing is great."

Clarity in the gospel must acknowledge this many-faceted vision for the gospel, or it will lead to division and factions; kingdom people fighting with cross people fighting with grace people. This brings up the other goal in unpacking this vision: unity for the church. Division between Christians (especially division between Bible-believing Christians) is tragic and sad. It betrays the very spirit of the gospel we proclaim.

We want to insist that there is one gospel, and that there are three aspects to the gospel that strengthen and inform one another. More than that, we want to challenge you to step into the life-giving comfort that this gospel proclaims, experiencing the fruit of that gospel as a part of everyday, ordinary, regular Christianity. Doing this requires two things: the Word and the Spirit.

The Word

To be sure, we're not simply advocating more Bible knowledge. We don't come to the Bible as if we were studying to pass the divine equivalent of the SAT. In fact, Jesus rebuked good church men of the first century who studied Scripture more intensely than anyone: "You search the Scriptures because you think that in them you have eternal life; and it is they that bear witness about me, yet you refuse to come to me that you may have life" (John 5:39–40).

You could properly reinterpret the above by saying, "If you're reading the Bible and not seeing Jesus, you're doing it wrong." Jesus is boldly declaring that the whole Bible is about him. Peter echoes this in 1 Peter 1:10–12. The whole Bible points to Jesus, that we might know him and see him as the center of all our hopes.

The goal of our study of the Word is not book knowledge, but personal knowledge—we want to get to know Jesus. It's by reading the Scriptures, experiencing the stories and hearing God's promises, that we can begin to get a sense of who he is, what he's done. It's also by immersing ourselves in the Scriptures that we can begin to see the wonder of the whole gospel.

The Spirit

We need more than good study to see the wonder of the whole gospel. We need a teacher who can open our eyes, someone who knows us deeply and can make the connections between the Word and our desperate hearts.

Jesus tells us, "The Helper, the Holy Spirit, whom the Father will send in my name, he will teach you all things and bring to your remembrance all that I have said to you" (John 14:26). As we wrestle with the teachings of Scripture, the Spirit is present and able to teach us, to bring our hearts and minds into a place of understanding.

The very name "Helper" is elsewhere translated "Comforter." By opening our hearts to the gospel, the Spirit of God gives us a comfort that overshadows any affliction, shatters any fear, and exceeds any earthly joys or pleasures. This is the power Paul spoke of when he told the Thessalonians, "Our gospel came to you not only in word, but also in power and in the Holy Spirit and with full conviction" (1 Thess. 1:5).

When the Holy Spirit takes hold of us, he ignites our hearts and illuminates the Scriptures, giving us an ever-deepening sense of the greatness of our salvation and the glory of Jesus who saved us. When Jesus opened the eyes of some of his disciples to the Scriptures, they said their hearts burned within them (Luke 24:32). Paul prayed that the Ephesians would have "enlightened" hearts (Eph. 1:18). Something greater than comprehension happens when the Spirit of God does his work of teaching us.

It's what our souls are longing for. The gospel isn't an abstraction. It's not a dusty piece of history. It's, as Paul says, "the power of God" (1 Cor. 1:18), a vibrant and life-altering announcement. It's where life as a Christian begins, and it's the message that sustains it from beginning to end. As we dig into the Word with eyes open to this glorious message, we pray, "Spirit of God, show me Jesus," and looking to him, we're transformed.

Map It

When we read God's Word, we need God's presence. What are often called "disciplines of the Spirit" are helpful, then, to bring ourselves before the Word in a posture of dependency and readiness. Only the Spirit can open our eyes to the whole gospel.

Here are some practical suggestions for disciplines of Word and Spirit. Obviously, these lists aren't comprehensive. They're merely starting places for engaging with the Word and Spirit of God with a readiness to see Jesus, to see his glorious gospel, and to have our hearts transformed.

Prayers of Preparation—for before Reading the Word

1. Open my eyes, that I may behold wondrous things out of your [Word] (Ps. 119:18; see Eph. 1:18).
2. Lord, search my heart with your Word. Reveal to me sin that is keeping me from experiencing life (Ps. 139:23–24).
3. O Lord, let my heart burn as I read your Word (Luke 24:32).
4. O Lord, let me not merely hear your Word, but let me live out your Word (James 1:22).
5. O Lord, let the Word of Christ dwell in me richly (Col. 3:16).
6. O Lord, help me to see Jesus as my King/Lord ruling over me, as my Savior/Redeemer saving me, and as my Lover/Friend present with me always!

Questions to Ask

- What does this passage say about who God is?
- What does it say about who I am?
- How does this passage reveal the aspect(s) of the gospel?

  - Does it point to our hunger for a king or reveal Jesus as King?
  - Does it point to our guilt, or show how God provides a substitute for our guilt?
  - Does it show our powerlessness, or show how God is single-handedly our Savior?

- Does this passage show how the gospel motivates, or, if it's a command, how can the gospel empower us to obey?

Other Suggestions

- Memorize passages that help you gain a whole perspective on the gospel.
- Pray through passages, asking God that you could see it and believe it more clearly, and that you could show it to a lost world.

- Journal and notate through your Bible. Make shorthand symbols for kingdom, cross, and grace, sketching them in the margins whenever you come across them. Work through a whole book this way (try Colossians) and then review.
- Meditate on the parables in the Gospels. Compare your desperation and dedication to that of the characters in the parable.

Passage Suggestions

1. Read Acts 20. It's jam-packed with Paul's missionary adventures. Notice Paul's language:

- "But I do not account my life of any value nor as precious to myself, if only I may finish my course and the ministry that I received from the Lord Jesus, to testify to *the gospel of the grace of God*." (v. 24)
- "And now, behold, I know that none of you among whom I have gone about *proclaiming the kingdom* will see my face again." (v. 25)
- "For I did not shrink from declaring to you the whole counsel of God. Pay careful attention to yourselves and to all the flock, in which the Holy Spirit has made you overseers, to care for the church of God, which he *obtained with his own blood*." (vv. 27–28)

In one conversation, Paul refers to his message as the gospel of grace and the gospel of the kingdom. He then implicitly refers to the gospel of the cross by naming the church the people bought by the blood of Christ. Paul was proclaiming one unified message, and he saw that the single message was multifaceted.

2. Read Luke 23:36–43:

The soldiers also mocked him, coming up and offering him sour wine and saying, "If you are the King of the Jews, save yourself!" There was also an inscription over him, "This is the King of the Jews."

One of the criminals who were hanged railed at him, saying, "Are you not the Christ? Save yourself and us!" But the other rebuked him, saying, "Do you not fear God, since you are under the same sentence of condemnation? And we indeed justly, for we are receiving the due reward of our deeds; but this man has done nothing wrong." And he said, "Jesus, remember me when you come into your kingdom." And he said to him, "Truly, I say to you, today you will be with me in Paradise."

The gospel of God's cross is the setting for this scene—Christ is literally hanging on the cross. He is referred to as a *king* and the criminal hanging next to him pleads for acceptance into Jesus's *kingdom.* Finally, Jesus promises this man he will enter paradise that same day. Though this man was condemned, Jesus extended grace and saved him. These verses show the whole gospel at work.

3. Read Romans 1:1–5:

> Paul, a servant of Christ Jesus, called to be an apostle, set apart for the *gospel of God*, which he promised beforehand through his prophets in the holy Scriptures, concerning his Son, who was descended *from David* according to the flesh and was declared to be the Son of God in power according to the Spirit of holiness by his resurrection from the dead, Jesus Christ our Lord, through whom *we have received grace and apostleship* to bring about the obedience of faith *for the sake of his name among all the nations.*

Themes of the whole gospel are italicized in the above verses. Paul has been set aside to preach the gospel of *God* (what is the whole gospel if not the gospel of God himself?). Jesus is descended from the great King David as the promised ruler whose kingdom would have no end. We are sent as representatives to the nations to proclaim the greatness of God's name. We aren't given this responsibility because we deserve it or have earned it, but rather as a gift of grace.

Part 2

The Whole Church

Introduction to Part 2

We often talk out of both sides of our mouth when we talk about the gospel and the church. We say that the gospel is the message that we can do nothing to save ourselves, while the church is defined by all the things we must do to be saved. The free gift of the gospel is proclaimed to a congregation that has strict rules about who's "in" and "out," and that sets up hurdles people must leap over if they want to count themselves as "in."

The result is a community with a shiny veneer and a rotten core. "Whitewashed tombs," Jesus called it, where the exterior of polish and togetherness conceals something that is falling apart on the inside. Outsiders and insiders alike fear attending the church because of wayward glances, judgment, and gossip. They fear backbiting and theological warring. A doctrinarian church lambasts the socially engaged church down the street for being shallow, and the latter retaliates against the frozen-chosen attitude that's kept the former stagnant for generations.

Choosing a church can feel a bit like walking into a Baskin Robbins. The flavors are endless, and far more than doctrine or leadership structures can separate them. We find wars over worship, small groups, Sunday school, social justice, and children's programs. National conventions for major denominations are often known not for the loving spirit of cooperation that they exude, but for the wars they fight.

Yet, standing over all the conflict and tension is the wonderfully simple and profoundly deep message of the gospel, that God has welcomed us into life in his kingdom, through his Son's cross and with scandalous grace. It's a message that gets lost when Betty and Petunia start duking it out over whether the carpet should be pink or pink, and when young punks start turning up the music until ears bleed.

What if, instead of starting with the all the external definitions of "church," we started with the internal definitions of the church—that the church is a population formed by the gospel. What if the conversation started there and flowed outward? What if the decisions we made as a church all had to come back to the centrality of that simple and deep message? What if the starting place for who we are as a church flowed first and foremost from the scandalous grace that meant we were free, that we had nothing to prove and nothing to earn?

The gospel invites us into a different way of living and being, not to prove or earn, but to enjoy. It's truly a better way and a richer kind of life, and the Bible gives us many clues as to what that life looks like. What we do as believers will always flow from who we are, and in Christ, we've been given a radical new sense of identity.

There's much talk in the church about "gospel-centered" ministry. The church is a gospel-centered and gospel-formed community, and we can most faithfully live out our purpose and mission when we cling tightly to the good news of God's kingdom, cross, and grace.

In the chapters that follow, we will unpack that gospel-formed identity in five aspects. We are worshipers, family, servants, disciples, and witnesses.[1] Each of these identities flows from the fact that God has welcomed us into his life through his Son, and each finds its fullest expression and definition in the person of Jesus. If the gospel is a map, then the identities—these ways of understanding what it means to be the church—are the highways and byways through the landscape. They are the roads we journey upon throughout the Christian life. The gospel takes hold of us and transforms us, and we live out new lives in the light of that glorious news.

5

Worshipers

At this very moment, and for as long as this world endures,
everybody inhabiting it is bowing down and serving something—an
artifact, a person, an institution, an idea, a spirit, or
God through Christ.

HAROLD BEST

When we encounter the gospel, we're fundamentally changed. The news of God's kingdom, cross, and grace is not simply a dot on the map, telling us of a location we may want to visit. It's an overlay—a new map that sits on top of the old map, changing everything about the way we live, the streets we walk, and the neighborhoods we inhabit.

At the center of this new reality is the reorientation of our hearts. What was once a cold, inward, and selfish stone is now a tender, living, flowering thing that cannot help but respond to the wonders it has experienced. As we've said before, it's not so much something new as the restoration of something very old: life the way God intended. We overflow in response to the gospel that has ignited our hearts, and the overflow itself is a testimony to the glory of God's gospel. *The gospel has made us true worshipers, and our worship is all about the gospel.*

Worship Wars

"Worship" can be a confusing word, and it's a topic that's fraught with conflict. Many who grew up in the church experienced the "worship wars"—years in which the "traditional" faction battled the "contemporary" faction over whether there would be drums and guitars in our gatherings.

While this is certainly the most familiar battle of the worship wars, it's not the only one. Those who may not battle over style may battle over substance or definition. You might attend a worship service on a Sunday, sing a song called "Here I Am to Worship," and in the same service hear a sermon about how worship isn't singing or services, but is actually all of life. Some of the attendees might say, "Since worship is all of life, I'm actually worshiping just as much when I'm at home watching football as I would be in church. So I might as well stay home." Others might say, "The Bible commands us to worship, to sing, and to lift our hands, so if I'm not participating in those things, I'm not actually worshiping."

So which is it? Is the Bible contradicting itself? Is worship all of life, or something that happens at a particular time and place on a Sunday morning?

A Much Older Worship War

To get to the bottom of these questions, we'll return to the Gospels. John 4 gives us a story in which Jesus deals with a worship war between Samaritans and Jews. In the opening verses, John tells us that Jesus and the disciples took a roadside break in Samaria. Jesus, resting by a well while his disciples go into town to buy food, meets a Samaritan woman and asks her for a drink. Their conversation leads to Jesus exposing her deepest, darkest secrets, revealing that she's been married five times and is currently unmarried and shacking up. Her response is to change the subject to the hot worship war being battled at the time.

> "Sir, I perceive that you are a prophet. Our fathers worshiped on this mountain, but you say that in Jerusalem is the place where people ought to worship." Jesus said to her, "Woman, believe me, the hour is coming when neither on this mountain nor in Jerusalem will you worship the Father. You worship what you do not know; we worship what we know, for salvation is from the Jews. But the hour is coming, and

is now here, when the true worshipers will worship the Father in spirit and truth, for the Father is seeking such people to worship him. God is spirit, and those who worship him must worship in spirit and truth." The woman said to him, "I know that Messiah is coming (he who is called Christ). When he comes, he will tell us all things." Jesus said to her, "I who speak to you am he." (John 4:19–26)

Jesus's response turns the question on its head, redefining what it means to be a worshiper.

The hot debate was, where is God going to meet us? Jews and Samaritans, long divided for a host of political, ethnic, and theological reasons, both believed they were worshiping the God of Jacob, and both believed that their particular brand of worship was the right way to do it.

They agreed that God was not someone whom you could take lightly. Because of this, they believed that his presence was available only at a particular time and a particular place, through specific actions led by a mediator like a priest.

This was how God had set things up with Israel. Sin had corrupted the relationship between God and man so that we couldn't be in his presence. And if God just showed up, it would go very badly for us. (If you've seen *Raiders of the Lost Ark* you know what we're talking about.) Indeed, when God showed up at Mount Sinai, lives were put in jeopardy, and all were warned: touch the mountain, and you die (Ex. 19:12).

Though sinners can't be in his presence, God, in his grace, provided a way of being with them. Through an elaborate ceremonial kind of worship, people could experience the presence and blessing of knowing God. They gathered on the Sabbath and gave animals as offerings to priests who sacrificed them inside the temple, as sin offerings. All of this was worship, punctuated by reading Scripture, singing psalms, and celebrating that God was present and among his people.

There was no question that the appropriate time for this was the Sabbath, the day that God set aside as holy, but the Jews and

The Whole Church

Samaritans disagreed about where the proper place to carry out the sacrifice was: Jerusalem or the mountain. Where is the right place to worship? Where is God actually going to show up to meet his people? It was a debate about time and place, but Jesus, when confronted with the debate, introduces a totally foreign concept:

> The hour is coming when neither on this mountain nor in Jerusalem will you worship the Father. . . . The hour is coming, and is now here, when the true worshipers will worship the Father in spirit and truth, for the Father is seeking such people to worship him. (John 4:21, 23)

In other words, worship as an event, worship confined to a time and place is going out the door, and spirit-and-truth worship is on its way in. Rather than worshipers seeking God on a mountain or at a temple, God is turning the tables: He is seeking worshipers, and they will worship in spirit and truth.

How is this possible? How can sinners handle the presence of the living God who once said, "Man shall not see me and live" (Ex. 33:20)?

Jesus Revolutionizes Worship

If you read the book of Hebrews, you'll discover that everything about time-and-place worship in the temple pointed to Jesus. The curtain that separated people from the Most Holy Place, where God dwelt deep inside the temple, was a sign for Jesus's body, through which we'd come into God's presence (Heb. 10:20). The priest who interceded on behalf of the people was a sign for Jesus, who now and eternally prays for us (Heb. 6:20; 8:1). The sacrifices, like bulls and goats, merely foreshadowed Jesus's own offering—his body (Heb. 10:4–5).

Jesus's surprising words to the Samaritan woman are about the gospel. Rather than requiring the right religious performance of us, Jesus himself perfectly performed all the religious work. He's the perfection and completion of everything that came before, and by doing it all perfectly, it's now finished, over, and done with. That's the heart of the gospel: Life with God (once available only through a perfectly performed and elaborate religious exercise) is available now, through the finished work of the Son, not because we've earned it or deserved it, but because he gives it freely to us through his glorious grace.

Spirit-and-truth worship, the kind of worship Jesus invites us into, is formed and fueled by the gospel. When the good news gets ahold of our hearts, by the power of God's Spirit, we're transformed. It's the Spirit that first makes us alive: "He saved us, not because of works done by us in righteousness, but according to his own mercy, by the washing of regeneration and renewal of the Holy Spirit" (Titus 3:5), and it's the Spirit who opens our eyes to see Jesus and know him: "But the Helper, the Holy Spirit, whom the Father will send in my name, he will teach you all things and bring to your remembrance all that I have said to you" (John 14:26).

As for the truth, it's probably not insignificant that elsewhere in the book of John, Jesus refers to himself as the truth. Worship is a reality experienced by the presence of the Holy Spirit and through the work of Jesus, who is the way, the truth, and the life (John 14:6).

Too often, we're like the Samaritan woman. When we think of worship, we think of locations, times, styles of music, personalities, and facilities. It's remarkable how often our judgment about the quality of a worship service is based on our preferences. Over the years at Sojourn, we've become really sensitive to that. Music at Sojourn is intentionally diverse, attempting to reflect the diversity of the congregation. One week may be straightforward indie rock, the next may be bluegrass or jazzy folk. The stylistic shifts inevitably lead to complaints, as we're almost guaranteed to be rubbing up against someone's preferences. "That wasn't good worship," someone will say, and we're quick to point out that, actually, they just didn't like the sound.

It's tempting in moments like this to respond as theologian Marva Dawn once did, when a church member complained to her about a particular song. "That's okay," she said. "It wasn't for you."

If worship is narrowly defined as a particular sound or style of music, Christians are stuck with a narrow and sadly limited vision. Jesus tosses the Samaritan woman's question on its head because he knows that these debates over methods are a distraction from our greatest need: an experience with the presence of God, something that isn't dictated by technique or location. Jesus offers us God's presence, and tells us that God is seeking worshipers. Not here or there, not with this or that style or technique, but in spirit and truth.

To fully understand what Jesus is making available, we have to return once again to the very beginning, where we'll discover that we are always worshiping, and we always were.

We're Always Worshiping Something

When God wired up the world, when he made Adam and Eve, he made them creatures whose lives were an exaltation. They exalted God—they honored him, worshiped him—with every moment of their lives. In the harmony of unmarred creation, their actions were echoes of God's own word for creation, "good." Everything was good, and everything Adam and Eve did in the midst of creation was an echo, a riff, an "amen" to that goodness. Harold Best calls this trait "continuous outpouring," and it's a great image.[1] Mankind was made to continuously outpour praise, responding to the glory and goodness around us through our lives and actions in the beautiful harmony of God's world.

When sin came to the world, it didn't cut off the valves of our outpouring; it redirected them. Suddenly the life and breath and energy meant to be in harmony with God's own words became a discordant, noisy sound. Mankind, the crown of creation, the only creature blessed as image bearers, was reduced to worshiping created things, lesser things, fallen things. We built lesser kingdoms and created false gods, false kings, who ruled over our broken world.

As Paul describes it, they "exchanged the glory of the immortal God for images resembling mortal man and birds and animals and creeping things" (Rom. 1:23). Isaiah's description reveals the absurdity of false worship:

He cuts down cedars, or he chooses a cypress tree or an oak and lets it grow strong among the trees of the forest. He plants a cedar and the rain nourishes it. Then it becomes fuel for a man. He takes a part of it and warms himself; he kindles a fire and bakes bread. Also he makes a god and worships it; he makes it an idol and falls down before it. Half of it he burns in the fire. Over the half he eats meat; he roasts it and is satisfied. Also he warms himself and says, "Aha, I am warm, I have seen the fire!" And the rest of it he makes into a god, his idol, and falls down to it and worships it. He prays to it and says, "Deliver me, for you are my god!" (Isa. 44:14–17)

Some false gods are made of wood. Some are bank accounts. Some are in our mirrors. False worship isn't limited to a few moments of slavish action toward a physical thing; it's a whole life apart from Jesus, an outpouring wasted on false kingdoms and false gods, even if that god is ourselves.

Writer David Foster Wallace, who wasn't a Christian, saw this reality at work in the world around him. He wrote:

In the day-to-day trenches of adult life, there is actually no such thing as atheism. There is no such thing as not worshipping. Everybody worships. The only choice we get is *what* to worship. And an outstanding reason for choosing some sort of God or spiritual-type thing to worship . . . is that pretty much anything else you worship will eat you alive. If you worship money and things—if they are where you tap real meaning in life—then you will never feel you have enough. . . . Worship your own body and beauty and sexual allure and you will always feel ugly, and when time and age start showing, you will die a million deaths before they finally plant you. . . . Worship power—you will end up feeling weak and afraid, and you will need ever more power over others to keep the fear at bay. Worship your intellect, being seen as smart—you will end up feeling stupid, a fraud, always on the verge of being found out. And so on.[2]

Wallace, who would later tragically commit suicide, illustrates the despair to which all false worship leads.

But Jesus transforms that reality. All of our failed efforts and misdirected worship are taken up in him, paid for by his blood, and forgiven. The whole mess of our lives is offered by Jesus to God, who in turn sees only the perfect life of Jesus and throws wide the gates of heaven.

At its best, time-and-place worship could only offer a brief interruption to otherwise sin-ravaged lives of false worship. Spirit-and-truth worship revolutionizes our entire existence.

Because of this, we are invited to boldly enter into God's once-terrifying, life-threatening presence (Heb. 10:22–23). We are living sacrifices (Rom. 12:1), a perpetual offering that God receives as acceptable because Jesus's own once-for-all sacrifice has made us acceptable (2 Cor. 5:14–15). Jesus transforms us into worshipers, making our every breath a "hallelujah," every exhale an "amen."

Worship: Gathered and Scattered

What we do with our lives, then, flows from who we are. We're transformed from false worshipers, slavishly worshiping false gods and kingdoms, into spirit-and-truth worshipers, offering our lives to God. Our worship now has two contexts, and each is shaped by the other. We worship gathered with God's people in community, and scattered as God's people in the world.

Gathering, for the people of God, is not an option. There is a temptation to take the concept of all-of-life worship and turn it into an apologetic for sleeping in on Sunday morning. After all, if all of life is worship, that includes sleeping in, drinking coffee, and watching *Meet the Press*, right?

In time-and-place worship, gathering was a necessary act, a narrow window of opportunity for meeting with God. Jesus's work of redemption throws wide the window of opportunity, but it doesn't abolish the call for the people of God to gather. Rather, the nature of that gathering is transformed. Instead of gathering for worship, we who are already and always worshiping now continue to gather in the midst of our worship. As Harold Best puts it: "We do not go to church to worship. But as continuing worshipers, we gather ourselves together to continue our worship, but now in the company of brothers and sisters."[3]

Gospel-Shaped Gatherings

The heart and purpose of our gathering, the story that gives it shape and focus, that gives our people hope and courage, must always be the gospel. The gospel makes us worshipers, and our worship, if it's to be meaningful and transformative, is all about the gospel. When we gather, we rehearse this story, seeing it displayed in bread and wine, hearing it in songs and sermons, singing it, and declaring it. It reminds us that our souls have an anchor, an immovable hope that sustains us through life's storms and prepares us for our inevitable return to the broader world, where storms await.

Early in the life of Sojourn, when we first came to see that the gospel needed to be at the heart of the life of our church, we had the "brilliant" and original idea of shaping our worship services in such a way that they walked through the rhythms of the gospel. "What if," we said, "we began our services with the idea that God has spoken and we are to respond? And then we walked through the movements of the gospel story: God is holy, we are sinners, and Jesus saves us from our sins. Then we sent people out in the light and power of the gospel?"

We thought we'd come up with something entirely unique. In fact, what we'd done is recreate the general movements of worship that Christians have been practicing for centuries. The word "liturgy" is often associated with a stylistic choice—services with chanting, reading, incense, and candles. In fact, liturgy simply refers to the idea that our service has an order, and in many of the great traditions of the church, the order of worship, the liturgy, was based on the story of the gospel.

Practically, this means that we first of all remember that worship starts with the God who created us, who speaks first to us through his Word and his Son, and who invites us to respond to him in worship. The gathering moves through the story of the gospel as a conversation then, where God speaks and we respond. The following chart gives a sense of what that conversation might look like.

The Whole Church

Rhythm	Gathered	Scattered
Call to Worship	Hear God's Word and respond to his glory and grace.	See each moment of your day as an opportunity to respond to God, no matter the circumstances.
Call to Confession	Let the Word and Spirit of God speak to your heart, revealing your sins.	Cultivate an awareness of your sin and need for grace in all of life, all of your relationships.
Words of Assurance	Hear God's promise that in Christ, you're forgiven.	Learn to preach the assurance of the gospel to yourself and others.
Passing the Peace[4]	Welcome strangers and newcomers.	Welcome strangers and newcomers.
Hearing God's Word	Cultivate an attitude of expectation for when God's Word is read and preached.	Seek out opportunities to hear God's Word.
The Lord's Supper	Sharing in the bread and wine is an opportunity to identify with Christ in his death and with the church throughout history, having gathered at that same table for two thousand years.	Share life with other believers. Share meals, share struggles, and share in the hope of the cross when you gather.
Commitment and Preparation for Sending	Respond to the preached Word with a commitment to live out the invitation of the gospel.	Invite others (Christians and non-Christians) to live out the invitation of the gospel.
Benediction	Recognize that in Christ you are blessed and sent.	Fill your relationships with the presence of Christ, and seek to leave those you encounter feeling blessed.

At Sojourn, this takes the general shape of:

A Call to Worship. God has revealed himself in glory and holiness, and we're invited to respond.

Responses (songs, readings, etc.) of Adoration. We respond in celebration of God's glory.

A Call to Confession or Lament. God's holiness reveals our sinfulness and the brokenness of our world. We are reminded when we gather that things are not the way they're meant to be.

Responses of Confession. We respond with a cry for mercy and grace.

Words of Assurance. Jesus meets us in our sin and brokenness and forgives our sins.

Passing the Peace. Just as Christ has welcomed us into his family, we welcome one another.

Preaching the Word.

Responses of Commitment.

The Lord's Supper.

Preparation for Sending. In the light of the gospel, we are called to go
and tell what God has done.

Responses of Commitment and Celebration. We proclaim what God
has done, and we celebrate his faithfulness as a body.

Benediction. A Blessing for the Road.

There's nothing magical about the above order, and it's not something
that is immovable; we regularly adapt elements according to the particular details of a given service. But it is a general movement, a chance
to soak in the rhythms of the gospel story, allowing it to confront our
sin and doubts and point us back to the Savior who reconciles us to
God and sustains us. It anchors us in the story of God becoming man,
enduring immeasurable suffering, and conquering all the great evils
of history. We're reminded of the great need in our hearts and in our
world while holding out the assured promise that one day all will be
made right once again.

The Gathering as an Outpost of Hope

The church that gathers comes in the midst of trials and suffering, like
a crowd that huddles inside a shelter to escape a storm. The author of
Hebrews tells us:

> Let us hold fast the confession of our hope without wavering, for he
> who promised is faithful. And let us consider how to stir up one another
> to love and good works, not neglecting to meet together, as is the habit
> of some, but encouraging one another, and all the more as you see the
> Day drawing near. (Heb. 10: 23–25)

The days are evil. The kingdom of darkness spreads its tentacles in the
world around us, wreaking havoc and wrecking lives. Whether it's cancer or divorce, miscarriages or house fires, domestic violence or political
corruption, the church is certain to face torrential downpours of suffering until Christ returns. We gather out of the ashes of a broken world
to hear the hope of the Word proclaimed and explained (Acts 2:42),
to feast on that hope through the Lord's Supper (Luke 22:19; 1 Cor.
11:24–25), to see that hope made real as the dead are brought to life

(Rom. 6:4), and to celebrate that redemptive work through the symbol of baptism (1 Pet. 3:21). We gather and we sing defiantly, refusing to let our hopes be crushed by the darkness around us (Col. 3:16). It's no secret that God's people have a long and rich history of singing together. The largest book of the Bible, often mislabeled as a prayer book, is a songbook: the Psalms. While it certainly is an invaluable resource for learning to pray, it's a kind of praying that's meant to be done with one voice as God's people gather, remember, and cry out to him in song.

This gathering is a foretaste, an outpost of hope that stands right on the edge of the "already/not yet" tension of history. The cross is the ultimate reconciling work of God (the "already"), but until he returns, we wait in what can be described as an in-between time (the "not yet"). We already taste the firstfruits of redemption, but we have not yet experienced its final, death-ending, world-unifying work. We are freed from the guilt and shame of our sins, but not from the presence of sin in our flesh and the daily battle against it. We are already citizens of heaven, but are not yet free from citizenship in whatever political institution holds authority over us. Death has lost its victory, but it still holds a power. Cancer wards remain, as do HIV clinics, mass starvations, famines, plagues, earthquakes, tsunamis, and genocides, but one glorious day these will all end. The hospitals, graves, and prisons will be emptied once and for all.

Until then, the church watches and waits, crying, "Come, Lord Jesus." And in the midst of its waiting, believers gather, acknowledging in one voice that Jesus is the true King and Lord, that death is defeated, and that one day all this madness will end. Jeremy Begbie calls worship an "echo from the future."[5] It's a sound we can hear right now that is not of this world. It's a foretaste of a time when all of creation will make that same confession with one voice, once and for all.

Remembering: The Fuel of Hope

The source of all hope, the fuel that sustains us, is the message of the gospel. Life with God is available now, through the finished work of his Son, not because of anything we've done but as a pure gift of grace.

From the moment God made a promise to his people in Israel, he commanded them to gather and remember together that promise. That remembrance continues in the church, which is commanded to gather to encourage one another, sustain one another, build one another up, and once again, remember the promise. And then, in the images we're given as we peek behind the veil of eternity with the apostle John in the book of Revelation, we see the people of God gathered around the throne, worshiping the slain Lamb (Revelation 5). Even then, when sorrows cease, God's people will gather and remember, worshiping the Lamb—the same Lamb foreshadowed in Israel's gatherings, in blood-stained doorways, in bread and wine in the gathering of the church, the Lamb slain from the foundations of the world (Rev. 13:8). The whole story, from beginning to end, is marked by the gathering of God's people, remembering their identity and celebrating God's promise together through songs, prayers, sermons, and feasts.

Gathering with God's people and remembering what he's done is not optional for the Christian life; it's a pulse-like rhythm that sustains us in community and focuses us on the gospel. Each gathering reminds us that the map of the work is demarcated by the kingdom of God. If the pulse stops, we will forget him and the life will drain out of us. From this gathering, we're sent back into the wider world, into the various avenues of our daily life, continuously outpouring and worshiping as we go.

Worship Scattered

There's a constant temptation to compartmentalize, seeing the gathering as a "sacred" moment while the rest of life is "secular."

Once Jesus's work on the cross is complete, the curtain between sacred and secular is literally torn down, leaving us to scatter into neighborhoods, workplaces, and homes with the awareness that our every moment is an opportunity to worship the God who sends us. Breakfast is a call to worship the God who made the sun shine on the hills where the coffee grew, who watered the orange groves and made the hens lay eggs. The morning commute is a call to confession as we face our impatience and frustration, or an opportunity to intercede for our broken world as we hear the morning news. A hurting coworker or brokenhearted child invites us to pass the peace to one another, and almost any conversation between spouses is an opportunity to assure one another of the forgiveness that's ours in Jesus Christ. How does this change the way we might interact with coworkers? How does it change our parenting? One morning, I (Mike) was leaving at 5:45 a.m. to go to the gym before work. Just as I put my shoes on, I heard my daughter crying. Still in the process of potty training, she'd wet the bed. I could have slipped out the door, and no one would have known that I'd heard her. I could have avoided dirty pajamas, soaked sheets, a crying toddler, and the inevitable task of smelling pillows, blankets, and stuffed animals to see which were clean and which were urine-soaked.

To do so would have been a strange sort of victory. My kingdom of self would have seen that as a pleasing offering, choosing the quiet of the morning and the fresh air over the dark house, tears, and unpleasantness inside. Instead, I chose to kick off my shoes, head to the bedroom, and wave my wife off the case so she could go back to sleep. Not because I love urine (which I don't). Not even so much because I love my wife and kids (which I do, very much). But because I couldn't help but see that moment as a chance to glorify God and live in the good of his creation. In the wonderful mystery of the gospel, a moment like this, of spraying sheets with stain remover, wiping tears, and changing pajamas, becomes a fragrant offering to our God. To do otherwise would have been to chose something small, something weak, something that's at its core deeply unsatisfying.

There is much more to say about the life of scattered worship. Much of that fills what remains here in this book, as we look at how the gospel transforms our hearts and gives us identities that, once lived out, point the world back to the gospel. Such a life is a living sacrifice, an every-moment reminder that we live in a different kind of kingdom with a much greater King than the other kingdoms that compete for our attention.

Such moments surround us, calling us to worship, to confess, to live out the gospel story in the varied moments of our days. Likewise, we're surrounded by the competing voices of a thousand lesser gods and their own destructive liturgies. It is these false gods, when worshiped, that destroy lives. If you want to discover them, look no further than your anxiety or fear. Lying awake at night worried about money? You're worshiping. Biting off your fingernails about a lack of recognition at work? That's your sacrifice of praise. Filled with rage for days at a time because of someone's harsh comment or backstabbing? There's a song of adoration going off in your head, and it's to your own name and reputation. Fear of God is the beginning of wisdom, as Proverbs 9:10 says, and it's a fear that displaces lesser fears and rightly orients us back to the one person in creation whose opinion matters, because he's the one who spoke creation into being and holds our breath in his hands. As we learn to sing his song throughout our days, the competition is revealed for its hollow emptiness.

True worship, spirit-and-truth worship, is a balm for anxious souls and hearts, inviting us to remember a story that's bigger than us, and a story in which all of the causes of our fear, anxiety, and tension are resolved. It's worship that is learned in community as we gather, hope, and remember—and practice throughout our days.

In this way, gathered worship and scattered worship work in dialogue with each other. The conscious, momentary gatherings where we remember our story in community serve as life-forming experiences, shaping the way our days and weeks are lived out. The days and weeks are filled with all kinds of challenges and troubles, and gathered worship punctuates them with an affirmation that in Christ, they're all held together and reconciled. Our scattered days fill with reasons to fear and sweat, which we bring to the church when we gather, only to hear them all held up and reconciled in Jesus and to be charged again to carry that reconciliation with us as we scatter.

In time, as we grow in grace, we learn to hold those things up moment by moment, and we experientially know the joy of all-of-life worship. The whole mess gets offered up, and Christ perfects.

The Whole Church

Map It

Who Am I?

The gospel makes me a worshiper, and my worship is all about the gospel. As a worshiper, I live a life that glorifies God the Father by the power of the Spirit and through the work of the Son.

Where Am I?

I am either worshiping idols, worshiping self, or worshiping God. If I worship idols, my life is oriented around them: the acquisition of more stuff, more status, or more security. If I worship myself, my life is all about me—my pleasures, my beauty, my reputation

True worship is a life lived to the glory of God. I worship both gathered and scattered, gathering as an outpost of faith in a troubled world to affirm what's true and encourage one another, and scattering to live a life of worship in my home, neighborhood, and workplace.

What Am I to Do?

Worship God, rehearsing the rhythms of the gospel both gathered with the church and scattered in the world. Recognize that joining my voice with the church gathered, as I sing, read, and confess with others, is an expression of unity and an opportunity to proclaim the gospel to those standing around me. Gathering for worship with the church is a way of reorienting myself to reality, where God is at the center of all things. Likewise, life "scattered" is an opportunity to make those same declarations and confessions to a watching world.

6

Family

I don't care to belong to any club that will have me as a member.

GROUCHO MARX

If the church is doing its job, it makes for a strange social club. Free grace, given as readily to the poor and hurting as to the well-pedigreed elite, doesn't result in hubs of exclusivity and privilege. Entrance paradoxically costs you everything—your entire life—and nothing—because Jesus has paid for everything.

The doors of grace have been thrown scandalously wide, welcoming sinners of all stripes to come together and revel at the glory of the Savior. As the old hymn says: "All the fitness he requires is to feel your need of him."[1]

In 1 Corinthians 6, Paul gives a list of those who are "out" of the club:

> Do you not know that the unrighteous will not inherit the kingdom of God? Do not be deceived: neither the sexually immoral, nor idolaters, nor adulterers, nor men who practice homosexuality, nor thieves, nor the greedy, nor drunkards, nor revilers, nor swindlers will inherit the kingdom of God. (1 Cor. 6:9–10)

But just when we might be tempted to get smug about the fact that we're "in," he adds:

> And such were some of you. But you were washed, you were sanctified, you were justified in the name of the Lord Jesus Christ and by the Spirit of our God. (1 Cor. 6:11)

The Whole Church

The church is a community formed by grace, which means that the members aren't accepted for their good credentials. Instead, we enter into and experience life with God, in his kingdom, by his grace—a community made possible only by the immense sacrifice of God's Son, Jesus. Those who think they have good spiritual credentials need not apply; the "righteous" are out, while those who are dry, broken, and thirsty, are in.

Grace leaves us free from the burden of past and future sins, and opens wide the door to a new way of being, to life with God and adoption into God's family—which includes all of our adopted brothers and sisters. The church is formed from a messy collection of people—convicted criminals whose sentences have been pardoned—and from the ashes of their broken lives comes a living and vibrant family. *Because of the gospel, we are now God's children, adopted into God's family.*

Who'd Want More Family?

Family is an elastic, ever-changing concept in our culture. When we were kids, the hit sitcoms on TV were shows like *The Cosby Show* and *Family Ties*. Today, TV families are marked by discord, divorce, and dysfunction. The Cosbys have been replaced by *Arrested Development*'s greedy and backbiting Bluths, while the Keatons have been replaced by *The Family Guy's* Griffins, who represent a smorgasbord of dysfunction. It's tempting to think, "We should protest! It's a war on the family." In reality, though, it's simply a more accurate reflection of how our culture sees the whole concept of family.

The truth is, most families are messy. As novelist Douglas Coupland describes it, "All families are psychotic."[2] Sin's curse has certainly spread its tentacles into our homes, and it corrupts everything it touches. Too many marriages end in divorce, and divorce brings with it a host of challenges to the hearts and minds of the children of divorcés. Statistics on sexual, physical, and emotional abuse for children are staggering, with 68 percent of sexual abuse victims reporting that the perpetrator was a family member.[3] It's no wonder that our distrust of family as an institution runs so deep.

No family escapes sin's fingerprints. Even in homes without abuse or divorce, it's inevitable that parents will wound their children, and vice versa. All families are sin-sick, all families are in need of grace, and all families are in need of a better hope than their own relationships.

This makes the gospel story all the more ridiculous. When God became flesh, he took a place in a human family with imperfect parents and siblings. You know the fear and trepidation you experience on the way to see extended family during holidays? God decided to willingly add that stress to Jesus's life.

But you'll be hard-pressed to find something Jesus touched that he didn't end up transforming, and family is no exception. Jesus redefined family in a radical way that speaks to both "good" families and "bad" families. He gives us a picture of a new way of being that ultimately defines who we are and how we relate to one another.

Family in Jesus's Time: The Family Code

The culture of family has changed quite dramatically since Jesus's day, and the gap of history softens some of his words. To feel their force and sense their strangeness, it's helpful to know a little bit about the world he inhabited. New Testament scholar Joseph Hellerman unpacks what we'll call the "family code," revealing the way that the community in the era of the first-century church viewed its relationships:

The first principle of the family code says:

> In the New Testament World . . . the group took first priority over the individual.[4]

Concretely, this meant that one would give deference to the group, particularly if that group was your family. Like Spock says in Star Trek II, "The good of the many outweighs the good of the one." For Spock, it was a matter of logic. For first-century families, it was a matter of loyalty.

Hellerman goes on to say: "A person's most important group was his blood family."[5] Loyalty was the highest virtue, and there was no greater crime than ignoring the will of the group or betraying it for another. The closest parallel, in terms of "group-first" thinking and family loyalty, in our day might be the Mob. In *The Godfather: Part II*, there's a famous scene where Michael Corleone discovers his brother's betrayal of the family. In a chaotic moment, Michael grabs Fredo by both sides of his head, and kisses him. "I know it was you, Fredo. You broke my heart. You broke my heart!" The sense of betrayal is powerful. Equally powerful is the retribution that is eventually paid out on Fredo and all of the family's enemies. You don't betray your own. You don't deny, abandon, or conspire against your family.

Such a sense of obligation was uniform in the first century. It was assumed that if your family wanted something of you, you would conform for the sake of the group. Hellerman gives many historical examples of people who put their lives on the line for the sake of the group.[6]

Perhaps the family code's most shocking distinctive is Hellerman's final point on the topic, where he says:

> The closest family bond was not the bond of marriage. It was the bond between siblings.
>
> Corollary 1—The central value that characterized ancient family relations was the obligation to demonstrate undying loyalty toward one's blood brothers and sisters.
>
> Corollary 2—The most treacherous act of human disloyalty was not disloyalty to one's spouse. It was the betrayal of one's brother.[7]

Today, it's generally assumed that there is a primacy to the marriage relationship when it comes to setting family priorities. In Jesus's day it was quite different. The most important relationship was between siblings.

Jesus Blows Up the Family Code

This family code makes Jesus's behavior in Mark 3 all the more odd. Jesus has a public conflict with his family, and it results in a new definition for family. The scene is set in verses 20–21: "Then [Jesus] went home, and the crowd gathered again, so that they could not even eat. And when his family heard it, they went out to seize him, for they were saying, 'He is out of his mind.'" A few verses later, in the midst of Jesus's teaching the crowd, his relatives show up:

> And his mother and his brothers came, and standing outside they sent to him and called him. And a crowd was sitting around him, and they said to him, "Your mother and your brothers are outside, seeking you." And he answered them, "Who are my mother and my brothers?" And looking about at those who sat around him, he said, "Here are my mother and my brothers! For whoever does the will of God, he is my brother and sister and mother." (Mark 3:31–35)

Jesus's behavior flies in the face of all the acceptable norms. Culturally, his primary "group" is his family, and his deepest loyalty should go to his brothers. They're all on the scene, asking him to leave the strange company he's in, and he dishonors them by refusing. He ignores the family code.

The situation must have been pretty intense. Jesus was a man who, for thirty years, had lived an ordinary life as a carpenter. It's true that Mary had seen the angel, and had experienced the strange wonder of his birth, but she had also changed his diapers, watched him grow up, and now saw him in the midst of increasingly bizarre circumstances. For his brothers, none of whom had experienced the miracles of his young life, things must have seemed even more strange. Stories were spreading through the region about Jesus's teaching, his ministry of healing and casting out demons, and his authority (Mark 1:27–28). They were likely thinking, "Jesus? Our brother?" They knew him as one of the family, someone they ate with, worked with, and kicked up dust around Nazareth with. Now, suddenly, he's a sensation, with swarming fans packed in so tightly that he can't even eat.

Jesus Refuses His Mother and Brothers

Jesus is doing strange things, making religious leaders mad, and not eating right. Mama decides it's time for him to come home and get his head screwed back on straight. When she shows up, Jesus delivers a blow that really hurts. "Who are my mother and my brothers?" (Mark 3:33). He's calling the group bond into question. "Where do I owe my loyalty?" he essentially asks.

It's a surprising moment: Jesus is wounding his family. He's wounding his mother and brothers, and yet we know that Jesus lived his entire life without sin. Sometimes in medicine, you have to slice open a patient to make him well, and the Great Physician here is carrying out surgery on his family for both their sake and ours. His actions here are not unlike his fury at the temple, where he overturned the money changers' tables and drove out the livestock. His fury there was a righteous fury, just as his indignant attitude was truly righteous indignation.

Jesus's motivation for wounding his family is the same motivation that was behind all he did in his life and death. "Whoever does the will of God, he is my brother" (Mark 3:37), he says, pointing to something bigger than the bonds of blood to define his relationships. His mission is to welcome sinners into God's kingdom, and no one—not the Romans, or the religious authorities, or even his own family—is going to be allowed to stand in the way of that mission.

The family has come with its own agenda for Jesus's life. Perhaps Mary doesn't want her son at the center of controversy, or perhaps she can't bear to see him suffering for the sake of these demanding crowds that press in on him. But Jesus won't allow his agenda or the Father's will to be defined by anyone else. Mary can't stand to see Jesus suffering. Like others in Jesus's life, she can't see the big picture, the grand miracle that's happening as he gathers sinners to himself. So Jesus, in a way that can be described as both mysteriously harsh and loving, wounds her that he might show them all a greater bond than flesh and blood.

"Whoever does the will of God" could mislead us. Our religious tendencies hear it and get ready to pounce on the opportunity to perform and prove. "I can be family! I can do God's will!" But God's will is a funny thing, particularly in regard to who's in and who's out of his family. He decided you and I were unfit for determining whether we had a place in it and took the whole business upon himself. So to do God's will is simply, as Jesus put it, to "believe in him whom he has sent" (John 6:29).

Adoption: Jesus Widens His Family

There's another way to understand this conflict. Mary and Jesus's brothers show up asserting, "Jesus, you belong with us." His response is to say, "No, I belong with whoever belongs to God." The "family" is standing outside of a building full of sinners, calling to the Savior, asking him to extricate himself and come back to a place of some decency or normalcy. Jesus says, "No, I belong in the mess, and so do you."

The beauty of Jesus's words to his family isn't that he excludes them, but rather that he throws the nets of his family wider than what they're comfortable with. "My family includes all the riffraff and troublemakers that belong to God." He won't cast aside these sinners in favor of more decent company. Grace knows no prejudice, no class, no judgmentalism over personal history. It says only, "You belong. You have a place. You have a home."

It's a radical redefinition of family, and it's echoed throughout the New Testament. With God as our Father, and Jesus as our Brother-in-Chief, we are adopted into the family of God: "For in Christ Jesus you are all sons of God, through faith" (Gal. 3:26).

New Testament scholar Russell Moore, who has written extensively on the doctrine and practice of adoption, paints a compelling picture to help us see how truly miraculous and wondrous our adoption is. He tells the story of adoptive parents who are about to take custody of a twelve-year-old child. The child, they're told, has been in and out of psychotherapy, is prone to violence, "acts out sexually," and comes from a family with a history of violence generation after generation. Moore says:

> Think for a minute. Would you want this child? If you did adopt him, wouldn't you keep your eye on him as he played with your other children? Would you watch him nervously as he looks at the butcher knife on the kitchen table? Would you leave the room as he watched a movie on television with your daughter, with the lights out?

> Well, he's you. And he's me. That's what the gospel is telling us. Our birth father has fangs. And left to ourselves, we'll show ourselves to be as serpentine as he is.
>
> That's why our sin ought to disturb us. . . .
>
> But the New Testament addresses former Satan-imagers with good news. It's not just that we have a stay of execution, a suspension of doom. It's not simply that those who trust in Christ have found a refuge, a safe place, or a foster home. All those in Christ, Paul argues, have received sonship. . . . All those who are in Christ have found a home through the adopting power of God.[8]

If we understand the gravity of our sinfulness, we'll discover that we're just like the assembly of sinners who so disturb Jesus's family. We'll take comfort from Jesus's strange and disturbing words as he refuses to leave, because it means he's welcoming us into that family. That adoption changes the way we view the world. No longer are we orphans, without a home, without a center, without a father to look out for us. Instead, we're children, with all the rights and intimacy that goes along with a father-child relationship.

> For all who are led by the Spirit of God are sons of God. For you did not receive the spirit of slavery to fall back into fear, but you have received the Spirit of adoption as sons, by whom we cry, "Abba! Father!" The Spirit himself bears witness with our spirit that we are children of God. (Rom. 8:14–16)

Not only that, we are told that this was God's plan—to adopt a gang of sinners into his family and make them coheirs of his kingdom with Jesus: "He predestined us for adoption as sons through Jesus Christ, according to the purpose of his will" (Eph. 1:5).

We might be tempted to ask why the language is all about sons, and not sons and daughters. Were the writers of the New Testament just misogynists? Here, a little background information is helpful.

Sonship in the New Testament

The culture to which the Bible was written was strongly patriarchal, and all the wealth, power, and authority of a family was passed from generation to generation through the sons. It was expected that daughters would marry, and their new family would be the source of any inheritance for their families. Sonship, then, was a privilege that promised an inheritance and a share in the authority of the father. When the Bible uses the word "son" to describe Christians, as opposed to the word "children" or "sons and daughters," it is once again doing something scandalous. It means that all Christians, male or female, are heirs to the great inheritance of Jesus, our King. As Paul says elsewhere: "There is neither Jew nor Greek, there is neither slave nor free, there is no male and female, for you are all one in Christ Jesus" (Gal. 3:28).

To put it in the terms of the gospel, Christ's work on the cross has made us all coheirs with Christ of God's kingdom, not because we've deserved or earned it, but because God has made it available through his radical, scandalous grace.

The gospel has united us in stature before God, each of equal worth and value because our worth and value are found in Christ and not in us. This is not to say that there aren't different kinds of callings and different roles to play in the life of the church and family—the Bible speaks to men as men and women as women—but in our essence, in our intrinsic worth, we are all gloriously and equally hidden with Christ in God.

Life in this family, then, is defined by that reality. It's a life that's marked by acceptance, commitment, and intentionality.

Acceptance: We Don't Choose Our Family

It's fairly easy to long for greener pastures when we think about family. As kids, there was always the "cool mom" or "cool dad" who was more permissive, or more understanding, or at least owned an Xbox. There were families that always gathered around the dinner table together, or who seemed to have impeccable bonds. Later in life, we envy children who obey, or in-laws who don't intrude, or wealthy, lottery-winning uncles. Behind the closed doors of our own families, we're forced to see the flaws and bear the burdens of one another's weaknesses.

The Whole Church

God's expectation for us is the same, and the New Testament shows us how family was formed in some pretty unexpected places.

The Murderer

In Acts 7, Stephen delivers one of the longest and most beautiful sermons in the New Testament. Stephen was a well-loved brother in the church, one of a group of leaders appointed in Acts 6, and clearly a magnificent preacher and passionate follower of Jesus. He finishes his speech and is murdered by an enraged crowd, worshiping Jesus aloud as the hate-filled mob screamed to drown him out and pummeled his body with stones. Nearby stood a man named Saul, nodding in approval.

In Acts 9, Jesus calls Saul from darkness to the blinding light, and this once-murderous torturer of the church is suddenly found weak and blind among Christians. Jesus's word to the church is to welcome him, heal him, and baptize him. Soon he's preaching and planting churches, and eventually, he's recognized as the Apostle to the Gentiles, one of the foundational pillars of the church.

Now imagine yourself as one of Stephen's friends. Imagine seeing this broken man, Saul, huddled and blind in the corner of Ananias's home. Imagine the rage you'd feel when you realize he murdered your friend. "Serves him right," you'd think. "He got what he deserved." Imagine how conflicted you'd feel when you heard him proclaim Jesus as Lord at the synagogue, and imagine how bizarre and upside down it would seem to see him preaching, writing, and planting churches. Martin Luther said:

> The gist of the Gospel is this: No man is so high or may rise so high that he need not fear becoming the lowliest. Conversely no one has fallen, or may fall, so deeply, as to preclude all hope of becoming the highest. For all merits are abolished here, and God's goodness alone is glorified. By saying: "The first shall be last" Christ takes all presumption away from you and forbids you to exalt yourself above any prostitute, even though you were Abraham, David, Peter, or Paul. But by saying: "The last shall be first" He guards you against all despair and forbids you to cast yourself under the feet of any saint, even though you were Pilate, Herod, Sodom, and Gomorrah.[9]

In the family of the church, it shouldn't surprise us that the murderer becomes the preacher, because it's all built on a foundation of grace. We all arrive at Jesus's feet empty-handed, and we all receive what follows as a gift.

In Sojourn's earliest days, I (Daniel) was struggling to see myself leading a community of Christians. I'd never seen a church or ministry that was truly open about sin. You'd hear a lot of talk about how "I used to struggle with this," or "I had to overcome that," but I'd never seen people who sinned "in the present tense." I'd certainly never seen a pastor who was transparent about sin and struggles. Yet I was thoroughly aware of my own present-tense sin. As the apostle Paul put it in Romans 7, my heart was eternally at war, doing the things I hate, unable to do the good I longed to do.

As God continued to open the doors and move Sojourn forward, I made it clear to anyone who came, to any who would listen, that Sojourn would be a church for the broken, a church where we all recognize that weakness comes before strength. I said that if Sojourn ever became a church where I couldn't fall apart in my brokenness, then it would be a church where I could no longer lead. I believe it's just that sort of community that Jesus drew to himself in the Gospels, a community of beggars and vagabonds that crowded around him and couldn't get enough.

Strange Company

Another example of such community comes from Luke 8, where we see a "roll call" of sorts of Jesus's followers:

> Soon afterward he went on through cities and villages, proclaiming and bringing the good news of the kingdom of God. And the twelve were with him, and also some women who had been healed of evil spirits and infirmities: Mary, called Magdalene, from whom seven demons had gone out, and Joanna, the wife of Chuza, Herod's household manager, and Susanna, and many others, who provided for them out of their means. (Luke 8:1–3)

Church tradition has long speculated that Mary might be the woman with the alabaster jar in the previous chapter, who, because of the great forgiveness she experienced from Jesus, anointed his feet with oil and wiped them with her hair. Others have speculated that she was a prostitute. The text tells us only that this woman had once been possessed by seven demons, and now she keeps company with God, Joanna, and Susanna. Most of the demon-possessed people we meet in the Gospels are social pariahs, living on the fringes of society and in deep darkness. Here, we see a former demoniac hanging out with women of means—the wife of a high-ranking official, and Suzanna, about whom we know little apart from her help in bankrolling Jesus's mission.

Murderers, wealthy financiers and, ex-crazy-persons all gather at the feet of Jesus. One ex-crazy-person later accompanies Jesus's mother to his grave; as a good Jewish woman, she should have known better (culturally speaking) than to keep such shady company. But the gospel illuminates the common thread of humanity, the common thread of sin, and the sole hope of Jesus to get us out of the mess we've made. Just as we're radically accepted by Jesus, we're called to radically accept one another, and just as Jesus's love toward us has been extravagant and generous, so must be our love for one another.

God gathers sinners from their disparate lives and backgrounds and unites them with a family bond that can never be broken, and the life they share then glorifies the God and gospel that saved them. God makes us a family, and our family is all about the gospel.

The Family at Sojourn

Sojourn's original campus is in Germantown, one of Louisville's historic urban neighborhoods. Like many urban neighborhoods, it's diverse, experiencing the tensions of gentrification as middle- and upper-middle-class folks move into the historic homes and update them, living next door to blue collar and working poor folks who have lived there for much of their lives. Along one border of the neighborhood is a train track, which separates Germantown from Smoketown. The track is a clear line of delineation between a predominantly white community and a predominantly African-American community. Any way you look at the community around us, the challenges for building community are clear: social and political, racial and economic.

Sojourn has a pretty basic structure. We gather large on Sundays and then scatter, meeting in homes for community groups throughout the week. From the start, we wanted to deliberately go to the other side of the tracks and build relationships, and we have been astonished over the years by the diversity that has emerged.

Community groups have street kids just getting off drugs sitting next to MDs. Groups are led by people who have come out of the underground rave scene, and are populated by college kids and retirees, blue collar and white collar, Democrats and Republicans. You can't help but look around the room and wonder, "What in the world do these people have in common?"

And the answer is Jesus. Only in Jesus can unity be found in diversity. Only in Jesus can a community's dividing lines be blended, faded, and erased. Only as we all come to terms with our own radical need for grace can we learn to extend that grace, openness, and welcome to others.

Commitment: We Stick with Our Family

Such diversity requires commitment. It's a certainty that broken people will hurt one another, and without a real sense of commitment to one another, there's no reason to suspect that community will last.

We live in a commitment-averse society. Single people are delaying marriage until later and later in life, and expectations for marriage are lowered. Whereas a few generations ago, careers were rooted in a company and workers had a strong sense of corporate loyalty, today people change jobs every few years. We avoid the burden of commitment at every opportunity.

Yet we celebrate a gospel that begins with a radical, unshakeable commitment toward us. As Jesus tells us:

> My sheep hear my voice, and I know them, and they follow me. I give
> them eternal life, and they will never perish, and no one will snatch

> them out of my hand. My Father, who has given them to me, is greater
> than all, and no one is able to snatch them out of the Father's hand. I
> and the Father are one. (John 10:27–30)

Through Jesus, God has promised to be there for us, to protect us, to let nothing separate us from him (see Rom. 8:29–30, 35–39). As he's promised to look out for us, he calls us to look out for one another. As James tells us: "My brothers, if anyone among you wanders from the truth and someone brings him back, let him know that whoever brings back a sinner from his wandering will save his soul from death and will cover a multitude of sins" (James 5:19–20).

This commitment is mutual. By committing myself to the church, I'm committed to a body of people that is, in turn, committed to me. Today in the church, this commitment is most often signified through what we call "membership," but at its core, it's a promise to look out for one another, a way of saying, "I'm in, I'm about this, and I want us to mutually journey together toward Jesus."

We resist making such statements because we love the sense of comfort and freedom we feel from a lack of commitments. At its heart, this sense of freedom is a mask for consumerism. It's an attitude that allows us to drift from church to church, from one big thing to the next, chasing fads and hype without setting down any roots. And without roots, we'll never go deep. We take and we take, and we never give, we never contribute, we never say, "I'm in."

As Pastor Joshua Harris says: "We've let proud independence keep us uninvolved. This can be pride that says, 'I don't need other people in my life.' Or it may be pride that says, 'I don't want other people to see me for who I really am.' Both forms cut us off from the blessing and benefits of community in the local church."[10] But we are deceived if we think we're free because we have no commitment. In reality, Christians who think they've made no commitments, who believe themselves free, are slaves to the worst kind of obligation: commitment to self. All of our personal histories should be enough to convince us that the First Christian Church of Me is a lousy place for accountability, encouragement, and support.

We need commitment because we're not free. We're not free from our sin-filled flesh, and unless we commit, unless we surround ourselves with people who have mutually promised to protect one another, we'll be forever enslaved to self. Something as simple as membership in a local church, a tangible and practical commitment to a body of believers, should be symbolic of a profound commitment. As Pastor Mark Dever puts it: "Church membership is not simply a record of a box we once checked. It should be the reflection of a living commitment or it is worthless. Indeed it's worse than worthless; it's dangerous."[11]

There may not be a chapter and verse in the Bible that says, "Thou shalt become a member in thine local assembly of believers," but in a culture of religious consumerism, faddism, and hype, we need to put down roots, demonstrate commitment, and submit ourselves to the practical accountability that church membership provides.

When we drift outside these connections, we deny what it means to be a family member. We drift off into our own inward, consumeristic way of living. Sometimes that's because of selfishness, sometimes that's because of shame, and sometimes that's because of conflict.

Selfishness

At our core, we're deeply selfish people, and life in the family of God will continually push against our selfish tendencies. Paul points to Jesus's own attitude as a reason to "do nothing from selfish ambition or conceit, but in humility count others more significant than yourselves. Let each of you look not only to his own interests, but also to the interests of others" (Phil. 2:3–4). Jesus's example of self-sacrifice wasn't merely for the sake of his own achievement, but for the good of the whole family of God.

As family, then, we're obligated to one another. The gospel should compel us to:

> Love one another, and try to outdo one another in showing honor (Rom. 12:10);

Live in harmony and associate with the lowly—those "beneath" our social status (Rom. 12:16);

Welcome one another as Christ has welcomed us into God's family (Rom. 15:7);

Bear each other's burdens (Gal. 6:2);

Sing to one another (Eph. 5:19);

Confess our sins and pray for one another (James 5:16).

Such encouragement could go much further. The beauty of "one another" statements is that they put us on both ends of the equation. The purpose of the many-membered family of God is to build up a broad base of life and experience. When I suffer, someone else who suffers can encourage me, and when I have joy, I can share that joy with those around me.

We are fools to think we can one-another ourselves. We need family around us. We need support in good times and bad because the days are evil and there is a hellish army intent on pulling us away from the hope we have in Christ. As the writer of Hebrews said: "Let us hold fast the confession of our hope without wavering, for he who promised is faithful. And let us consider how to stir up one another to love and good works, not neglecting to meet together, as is the habit of some, but encouraging one another, and all the more as you see the Day drawing near" (Heb. 10:23–25).

Shame

Shame is a second reason we stay away from the family. Like our father Adam, we attempt to cover ourselves with fig leaves—shoddy and desperate attempts to hide our sin and need. We pose and pretend that life is great, posting tweets and status updates that put our best foot forward, somehow thinking that if the world thinks we're happy and great, it'll make us feel better. In reality, what we need is to be known and loved just as we are—just as God has known and loved us.

Shame has deep and powerful roots in us, whispering fearful things into our minds when we think about drawing near to God's family and really letting people into our lives. We're experiencing shame whenever we:

Feel bad about who we are;
Aren't comfortable in our own skin;
Live in fear of being found out;
Worry, "If you really knew me, you'd reject me."

Who would want his every thought and deed displayed on his forehead? No one. Sin is awful, and it's no coincidence that it results in shame. Shameful things tend to do that.

But the good news is that Christ brings a spirit of love and acceptance into the church. Just as we've been wholly accepted by God, in Christ, we can wholly accept one another. The shame we feel is shame we share—we're all sinners in desperate need of grace—and the cross is where our shame is laid bare and taken away from us. John says:

> So we have come to know and to believe the love that God has for us. God is love, and whoever abides in love abides in God, and God abides in him. By this is love perfected with us, so that we may have confidence for the day of judgment, because as he is so also are we in this world. There is no fear in love, but perfect love casts out fear. For fear has to do with punishment, and whoever fears has not been perfected in love. We love because he first loved us. (1 John 4:16–19)

It's worth noting that there's a difference between a gospel-driven authenticity and the kind of brash and cold authenticity that we often see in the world around us. Some, in the name of authenticity, adopt a harsh "you have to accept me as I am" attitude, making no apology for faults and sinfulness. The gospel, while it frees us from the burdens of our sin and shame, never excuses us. Our sin results in Christ's death, which both calls for us to be humbled by our sin and frees us from the burden of shame that once accompanied it.

There's no need for shame in the family of God because God has resolved cause for shame in the terribly fearsome things he's done to Jesus. Now there is only love for his children, and anyone in the church who preaches or acts otherwise is in a sad state of denial. We all come to Christ as beggars for mercy, and he covers our shame with his dignity, glory, and grace.

The Whole Church

Conflict

The final (and perhaps most challenging) reason we avoid the family of God is conflict. Many, after years in the church, decide that it's not worth the pain and risk of being burned and hurt once again. But being conflict-free has never been a biblical promise.

The Bible calls Christians ministers of reconciliation (2 Cor. 5:18–20), and points to the gospel as the reconciling power of the universe. God has eliminated the sin problem between him and us, and he expects that same power to eliminate the sin problem between him and us. Jesus expects the same (Matt. 5:23–24), and John says, "If anyone says, 'I love God,' and hates his brother, he is a liar; for he who does not love his brother whom he has seen cannot love God whom he has not seen" (1 John 4:20).

As Sojourn was forming, we adopted "bold love" as one of our core values (a phrase we borrowed from author Dan Allendar's book of the same name). We defined it as "loving someone enough to talk to them, not just about them." It was, in part, our own reaction to the conflict and gossip we'd seen rip through the churches of our youth like derailed freight trains. The Bible, we recognized, presupposes that conflict will occur. The question is about how we'll deal with it.

The two of us have been in ministry together now for more than a decade, and that's been a shock to some people. It's even more shocking when they discover that we're still friends, apart from work, apart from responsibilities. "How do you do years of ministry together and remain friends?"

It's certainly not that we haven't fought (loudly, publicly, and regularly). But early on, we determined that we'd work things through. We regularly confess sin to one another—even embarrassing sins about brooding over conflict or hurt feelings. We seek forgiveness when we fail to defend the other person or when we fail to cut off gossip about one another. Very early in the life of Sojourn, we made the commitment, "I've got your back," and it's a phrase that's stuck with us the whole journey.

Conflict is sure to emerge. People, pressure, and life circumstances are determined to drive us apart, and temptations abound for people to bail on ministry or church for the same reason they bail on anything in life: it's hard. We fought for unity, even to the point of getting counseling to help manage our relationship. It takes long, challenging work to maintain friendships in a setting where conflict is certain, but the gospel makes it possible, and makes it a priority.

Conflict in the church is a universal reality, but the power of grace should be transforming us in such a way that we see reconciliation as being truly better than holding a grudge. Remember that the gospel begins with terrible news—we're desperately sin-sick—and without that foundation, the good news means little. The bad news is universal, so those with whom we have our conflicts are neither more in need of grace than us or less so. This includes pastors, pastors' wives, deacons, old people, young people, angry people, complacent people, and malicious gossips. We're all in the same boat, floating on a sea of grace. The result of knowing this is a powerful boldness to be honest, weak, and truthful as we seek to resolve our conflicts.

Unresolved conflict fails to recognize the breadth of the gospel's power to reconcile us to one another. Shame fails to recognize that Jesus's finished work eradicates any cause for fear. Selfishness fails to acknowledge that the gospel is a message that should compel us to see beyond the ends of our own noses. But the gospel forever speaks of a different way. It meets us where we are, broken and orphaned, and it transforms us. Jesus pays the astronomical cost of our adoption, and through him we're made coheirs with him of God's kingdom. Together, we share life with God, and the life we share glorifies the God who rescues us. The gospel makes us family, and our family is all about the gospel.

Intentionality: We Discipline Ourselves for Community

Our commitments are only as real as the steps we take to ensure that we keep them. If we're going to have a vibrant life with God's family, we need to be intentional about the commitment we've made. Think of intentionality like a discipline. Disciplines are things we choose to do with regularity to help us live in ways that we otherwise wouldn't. So running daily, unless you're an escaped convict, is a discipline. Likewise, intentionality, in community, is a discipline; it's a way we choose to live that would otherwise be unlikely.

Most of us, if the world around us is any indicator, are unlikely to break outside of our cultural, social, racial, and economic spheres for relationships. But as I hope you'll now agree, being the church is an invitation to do just that.

It would be strange to meet someone who said, "Yeah, I love my family. But I never ever see them." You'd know that something was wrong. "Do they get together?" you might ask. "Sure, all the time, but I don't meet with them. I'm a Robinson, but I don't have to get together with the other Robinsons. I can be a Robinson just fine by myself." Others might be a bit more involved, but they only show up when the family's headed out somewhere good for dinner and Mom and Dad are picking up the bill.

Both cases show someone who—possibly for legitimate reasons— is living outside of a family identity. To be a family member means living intentionally. It means working hard to build and maintain connections to the family: family meals, family gatherings, family care. It means giving your presence to those around you and living out gospel-transformed relationships in regular rhythms of gathering, serving, praying, and encouraging one another. In some seasons, it will demand that you're a listener and encourager, that you press into people's lives as they suffer or struggle; and in other seasons, others will do the same for you.

Family is an extraordinarily confused and troubled topic today, but nothing is untouched or unredeemed by the story that God is telling. No one should be journeying down the roads of God's kingdom alone. The gospel makes us a new family, and that family is a foretaste of something beautiful, a day when we'll all gather around the table for a feast with Dad, a feast hosted in honor of Jesus, our Brother, who went to unimaginable ends to bring us home. We live out our identity as family now, knowing that these rag-tag collections of former (and current) thieves, swindlers, addicts, prostitutes, liars, stumblers, and ne'er-do-wells all share a spectacular hope, inheritance, and future.

Map It

Who Am I?

The gospel makes us family, and our family is all about the gospel. I'm a child of God in the family of God.

Where Am I?

There are three possible responses here. You are either committed, casual, or cut off. If you are cut off, it's either because you have never really trusted in Jesus and joined the family of God or because you deny your faith by your actions through rejecting God's church. Nowhere does the Bible show us an individualistic faith where Jesus is only your personal Savior. This isn't just about going to church; this is about being faithful to the gospel. We're saying that the commitment that God has made to us through the sacrifice of the Son results in commitment to one another and sacrifice for another. Great families call for great commitment and great sacrifice.

What Am I to Do?

Living as the family of God can take many expressions. One expression that we play out within Sojourn is called community groups. A community group is simply a place where we seek to live out our identity as family. At community groups, we gather weekly to share life, talk about our journeys, and pray together. This often involves discussing questions that reflect on the week's sermons, though some groups will do specific book studies together. One of the beautiful things about community groups is their diversity. In most groups, you'll find a diverse sampling of the church's population—a varied mix of people from different social and economic strata. In a world that tends to be bitterly divided on those lines, it's a beautiful thing to see.

Another expression is in triads, or accountability groups. Here, two to three people get together to ask one another pointed questions and spur one another along. These groups encourage one another in prayer and study, and they guard one another against sin and temptation.

Overarching these groups is membership. We are called to form committed, intentional relationships. Committed, intentional membership communicates that the gospel is something that matters. This is an aspect of our gospel-informed identity that's worth organizing my life around. This isn't just a compartment of my life. Christ came into our world and was crucified and resurrected so that we could know God and live in interdependent relationships with one another in community. Christ sets before us life with him, his kingdom, where the focus is not ourselves. We're freed from having the world revolve around our little soap opera, and we're called into the far bigger drama of God's kingdom.

7

Servants

In the upside-down kingdom, true greatness is found in the
servant's kneeling with the basin and the towel.

MICHAEL CARD

We love underdog stories. Whether it's on *Friday Night Lights* or the
movie *Dodgeball*, we love seeing the little guy or a character everyone's written off take the victory. We cheer as the underdog overcomes
adversity and beats astronomical odds, often overcoming forces that
seem utterly overwhelming.

Perhaps this is because we all have a hunger for the gospel hidden
somewhere in our hearts. Think of the way the gospel story unfolds:
Darkness takes root in God's world, and God sets out to redeem it. He
powerfully floods the whole earth, but that's not the victory. He rescues Israel from slavery in a spectacular way, but that's not the victory.
Israel becomes a glorious kingdom, conquering all of her enemies, but
that's not the victory. Instead, God brings about world-changing salvation when a young, unimportant Jewish girl gives birth to a baby of
mysterious paternity. He's not a conqueror or scholar, he's a carpenter
who recruits his followers from common people—fishermen, house-
wives, and tax collectors. They don't rise up and become an army,
instead, they suffer and die—first Jesus, then his disciples. And yet his
sacrifice is the hinge of history, shaping everything before and since in
relation to his execution.

The gospel is the greatest underdog story ever told. As Pastor
Tullian Tchividjian puts it, "In God's upside-down economy, the road

to the top is from the bottom—and that flies in the face of everything our culture believes is necessary to be successful."[1]

Through a handful of relatively unimportant people who suffered, served, and died, God changed the world, making himself available to you and me and setting a trajectory to make all things new. When Jesus takes hold of our hearts, he plants that same underdog spirit in us, inviting us into a life where we discover that everything about how the world sees greatness is backwards, that it's truly better to serve than be served, to give than receive, to be lowly rather than great. This underdog spirit is a new identity: the gospel makes us servants, and our service is all about the gospel.

This was a lesson mostly lost on the disciples during Jesus's lifetime. Like us, they were tempted to see Jesus as a means to their own advancement, and they looked at their years of service and learning as steps up a hierarchical social, spiritual, or political ladder. As we explored in chapter 2 on the gospel of the cross, the disciples were often found arguing among themselves about who was the greatest, or who would be seated next to Jesus when he came into his kingdom.

This attitude is echoed in our hearts and churches today. We jockey for power in whatever context we find ourselves. We demand the platform in worship ministries; we demand leadership in small groups and Bible studies; we cling to leadership and hunger for recognition.

Our Me-First Milieu

Of course, this attitude isn't limited to the church. It's the way our whole culture works. Nonprofits know that if you can provide a platform for people to get public recognition for their generosity, donations will dramatically increase. TOMS Shoes donates a pair of shoes overseas for every pair sold, which is both truly generous and brilliant marketing. If you buy a pair of TOMS, you not only get shoes that are "in style" for this moment, you get a share in TOMS's image of generosity. They're not just selling shoes; they're selling a compassionate self-image. There's something self-congratulatory about it. There's something in it for you.

Social media has exploded our narcissism. "Facebragging" has become a new slang term for the way that social media has enabled us to shamelessly self-promote, self-congratulate, and generally make public fools of ourselves. As Jean Twenge and W. Keith Campbell, authors of *The Narcissism Epidemic*, have pointed out, there's a kind of democratization on the web, where everyone's opinion has been elevated (or deflated) to a common level. Journalists who fight to present information with clarity and objectivity find themselves contradicted and shouted down by raging bloggers and commenters with no actual knowledge of whatever circumstance they may be reporting. Self-expression on the web has led to a sense of entitlement, a belief that "everybody's opinion is just as valid as everyone else's."[2] Andrew Keen refers to the phenomenon as "ignorance meets egoism, meets bad taste, meets mob rule."[3] It's a world where the way up is to be louder, more flashy, more harsh and outspoken.

Our celebrity culture magnifies this narcissism. LeBron James has "Chosen One" tattooed across his shoulders. Donald Trump declares everything he does as the best, whether it's his steaks, his brand of bottled water, or his show, which he recently said was the "number one show on TV" in spite of the fact that no Nielsen rating or critic would agree with him. Movie director Lars Von Trier, while responding to criticism of his latest work at the Sundance film festival, blurted out, "I'm the greatest director in the world." When asked to clarify what he said and why he said it, he replied, "I don't have to justify myself. I make films and I enjoy very much making them. You are all my guests, it's not the other way round. I work for myself and I do this little film that I'm now kind of fond of and I haven't done it for you or the audience so I don't feel I owe anyone an explanation."[4]

The Quest for Affirmation

Behind it all is a sad and desperate need for validation. Our sin-scarred souls can feel their weakness and emptiness, and we search high and low for something to tell us that we're okay. Social media becomes a place where we can display how put-together we are. We can face-brag about our parenting skills, our wonderful marriages, and our great churches and friends. People who share our perspectives pour out affirmation, which is essentially back-scratching. It's a sort of social contract—we narcissistically display our lives on Facebook and Twitter in anticipation that our "friends" will affirm us, knowing that we owe them the same back-scratching and praise. But it's all hollow. It will never be enough.

What we need is an end to the quest for affirmation, an encounter with God that tells us that we're okay, that we have enough, that there's nothing left to prove. When the gospel impacts our lives, we're given an identity and affirmation that should forever eliminate the need to posture or facebrag. Because God has forgiven our sins, called us his children, and welcomed us into his family, we have the ultimate seal of approval stamped on our hearts. We don't need anyone to tell us we're a good parent, student, worker, artist, or person, because the only opinion that ever mattered looks at us and sees only Jesus: "Your life is hidden with Christ in God" (Col. 3:3). All of his obedience, perfection, performance, and glory are accepted on our behalf. While the world clamors for position and place, we can rest in the embrace of our Father.

Apart from God's liberating love, we're destined to make our lives and service about ourselves. Like worship, serving is an inevitable reality. As Bob Dylan put it, "You're gonna have to serve somebody."[5] We are in constant service to something because God has wired us up to be servants. Our quests for affirmation are an attempt to fulfill a God-given purpose and desire. Life apart from him is an endless attempt to validate our broken souls, a relentless and fruitless effort of self-service. We wallow in self-service, in grasping attempts to climb some invisible social ladder, but it's never enough.

This is the world into which Jesus came. It's a self-congratulatory, power-jockeying place. He came with the full approval of the Father, laying aside glory and demonstrating a radical freedom to serve which is revealed as a far more satisfying way to live.

The Servant at the Last Supper

There is probably no better picture of Jesus's selfless service than the story in John 13. It's Jesus's last night with the disciples, and even as he faces the looming shadow of death, he puts on a display of selfless, sacrificial service.

> Now before the Feast of the Passover, when Jesus knew that his hour had come to depart out of this world to the Father, having loved his own who were in the world, he loved them to the end. During supper, when the devil had already put it into the heart of Judas Iscariot, Simon's son, to betray him, Jesus, knowing that the Father had given all things into his hands, and that he had come from God and was going back to God, rose from supper. He laid aside his outer garments, and taking a towel, tied it around his waist. Then he poured water into a basin and began to wash the disciples' feet and to wipe them with the towel that was wrapped around him. He came to Simon Peter, who said to him, "Lord, do you wash my feet?" Jesus answered him, "What I am doing you do not understand now, but afterward you will understand." Peter said to him, "You shall never wash my feet." Jesus answered him, "If I do not wash you, you have no share with me." Simon Peter said to him, "Lord, not my feet only but also my hands and my head!" Jesus said to him, "The one who has bathed does not need to wash, except for his feet, but is completely clean. And you are clean, but not every one of you." For he knew who was to betray him; that was why he said, "Not all of you are clean."
>
> When he had washed their feet and put on his outer garments and resumed his place, he said to them, "Do you understand what I have done to you? You call me Teacher and Lord, and you are right, for so I am. If I then, your Lord and Teacher, have washed your feet, you also ought to wash one another's feet. For I have given you an example, that you also should do just as I have done to you. Truly, truly, I say to you, a servant is not greater than his master, nor is a messenger greater than the one who sent him. If you know these things, blessed are you if you do them." (John 13:1–17)

The key to the whole passage is the first sentence: "Having loved his own who were in the world, he loved them to the end." Jesus radically displays God's love by becoming a servant.

The book of Luke has a parallel passage to this story. While Luke doesn't include the foot-washing incident, he does include Jesus's dinnertime lesson about servanthood, and he gives us a window into the conversation preceding Jesus's teaching:

> A dispute also arose among them, as to which of them was to be regarded as the greatest. And he said to them, "The kings of the Gentiles exercise lordship over them, and those in authority over them are called benefactors. But not so with you. Rather, let the greatest among you become as the youngest, and the leader as one who serves." (Luke 22:24–26)

Luke's account shows that even in the sunset hours before the cross, the disciples had yet to understand Jesus's profound message about true greatness. As he marches toward the greatest act of service and sacrifice in history, they quibble about seating arrangements in the coming kingdom. As he prepares to suffer under the authority of a Roman tyrant, they argue about who among them will dominate the others.

"The way down is the way up," Jesus essentially says, getting on his hands and knees to scrub their filthy feet.

Why Footwashing?

Footwashing was a common practice in Jesus's day. Roads were just dirt, and these men would have worn sandals of rope and leather. Combine the sweat-inducing heat with nearly bare feet, and dusty roads, and you can imagine the result. When you entered someone's home, you came with filthy, sweaty feet, and it was common courtesy to have a servant wash them when you entered the home. Old Testament scholar Andreas Köstenberger notes: "The practice of footwashing, which has a long Old Testament tradition, usually was performed by slaves. In the present instance, however, Jesus stoops to perform this role."[6]

Some rabbis taught that this task was so lowly and demeaning that it was unacceptable to have a Jew do it—even if he was a slave. Even today in the Middle East, feet are considered filthy and undignified. You may have seen scenes from political protests where angry mobs pound statues or billboards with shoes, or you might recall the

Iraqi journalist who threw his shoes at a visiting president. It's considered a profound insult. There's a deep sense, culturally speaking, of disgust about feet.

On the night in the story above, it appears that something of a faux pas has taken place. Jesus was an important figure, a well-enough known teacher, that a crowd gathered and made quite a scene on his entry to Jerusalem. And yet, here he is, the guest of honor in someone's home, and no one has washed his feet. Not even his disciples considered their master's dignity and comfort at the meal. So as they bicker about their roles in the coming kingdom, he gets up, disrobes, assumes the role of a slave, and begins washing the disciples' feet. Songwriter and author Michael Card describes the moment beautifully:

> This is a pivotal moment . . . in that Jesus finally gives up on words. He has told them numerous parables about slaves, now he will portray the most humiliating of slave roles, the washing of feet. Even after three long years of his often bizarre and indescribable behavior, the disciples are befuddled by the inappropriate behavior that leaves them speechless.[7]

Only someone with nothing to prove could take such a posture. It's nearly impossible to imagine a Kardashian, an NFL star, or a head of state doing any such thing; it would be too disruptive to their image of power and prestige.

Yet Jesus, who has power and authority over everything on earth, is free to be radically sacrificial and to act like a slave, crawling on his hands and knees among a bunch of filthy feet. Only someone with the ultimate sense of affirmation, a sense that only the opinion of One mattered, could have such humility.

The Objection

As Jesus passes among the disciples, washing their feet, they are bewildered. Peter objects to the indignity of it all. "You shall never wash my feet," he says. His first response to Jesus is to say that Jesus is too good to wash his feet. Jesus replies, "If I do not wash you, you have no share with me" (John 13:8).

The Whole Church

They had just been arguing about who would sit where in the coming kingdom, and Jesus is telling them, "In my kingdom, the King is a slave. If you can't handle that, then you don't want my kingdom."

Peter then swings the pendulum in the other direction. "Lord, not my feet only but also my hands and my head!" (v. 9). There's more than a hint of religiosity in there. Not content to merely receive what Jesus has offered, Peter one-ups him, asking for a greater cleansing, demonstrating (as Peter often does) a desire to stand out from the crowd, to be exceedingly good at his religion.

But this moment isn't about Peter; it's about Jesus, demonstrating to the disciples (and to all of history) that the greatest among us is the one who serves out of deep and abiding love, out of a love that overflows from the love-filled community of Father, Son, and Holy Spirit, pouring out from them into the community of people made new by the power of the gospel. He says, "What I'm doing for you is enough." We need only to receive what Jesus has done—nothing more. No need for outdoing, one-upping, or adding on.

The Invitation: Serve and Be Blessed

Jesus ends his act of service with a lesson:

> Do you understand what I have done to you? You call me Teacher and Lord, and you are right, for so I am. If I then, your Lord and Teacher, have washed your feet, you also ought to wash one another's feet. For I have given you an example, that you also should do just as I have done to you. Truly, truly, I say to you, a servant is not greater than his master, nor is a messenger greater than the one who sent him. If you know these things, blessed are you if you do them. (John 13:12–17)

It's a fierce rebuke to the posturing, demanding, self-serving chatter of the disciples, and it's a fierce rebuke to the same self-serving chatter in our lives. "Don't you get it?" Jesus is asking. "If I'm your Teacher, then you need to realize that you'll never be 'greater' than me, and I just took on the task that a slave would feel undignified in carrying out. In my kingdom, the King takes on the role of the slave. If you want to follow me, then do as I do." Notice the last phrase: "Blessed are you if you do them." It's an invitation: Come and discover the joy of serving.

In the midst of our clamoring for power and recognition, Jesus says, there's a better way. Paul David Tripp puts it like this:

> Our culture feeds us the lie that the main goal in life is to climb the ladder of power and influence . . . but Jesus says that all those things are found in descending. Jesus and his kingdom are on a collision course with the values of this fallen world and he is calling us to align with him.[8]

We're just as clueless as the disciples. Our lives are just as focused on self-exalting and glory-grabbing. Honestly ask yourself: How do you define greatness? How are you clinging to attention and recognition?

Today, just as in Jesus's day, greatness means power, position. It means people serving me, and Jesus says a resounding, "No!" As an old Puritan prayer says so eloquently, we need to learn to pray:

> Let me learn by paradox that the way down is the way up, that to be low is to be high, that the broken heart is the healed heart, that the contrite spirit is the rejoicing spirit, that the repenting soul is the victorious soul, that to have nothing is to possess all, that to bear the cross is to wear the crown.[9]

This isn't some recipe for earning God's approval. We could never follow it well enough to do so. Instead, it's an invitation to a better way to live. God's approval is the starting place of our relationship with him—you're already approved and accepted. Living as a servant isn't a penance; it's an invitation that promises a reward. By serving, we'll discover a soul-satisfying and blessed way to live.

The gospel makes us servants, and as we live out that identity, our service is a testimony to the greatness of the gospel. Being a servant flows from the work of the gospel and reveals the goodness of the gospel to the eyes of the watching world. We serve God, who has gifted us to serve and invites us to serve all.

The Whole Church

Servants of God

Jesus can take joy in washing his disciples' feet because he has a greater vision than the humiliation of the moment. Ultimately, Jesus is living his life on earth for the glory of the Father, and by confronting the upside-down world of the disciples, he's putting on display the glory of God. It's his God-sized vision that frees him (and us) to God-sized service and sacrifice. He invites us to follow him into his Father's world, where it's better to serve than be served, and where our service is ultimately for him:

> When the Son of Man comes in his glory, and all the angels with him, then he will sit on his glorious throne. . . . Then the King will say to those on his right, "Come, you who are blessed by my Father, inherit the kingdom prepared for you from the foundation of the world. For I was hungry and you gave me food, I was thirsty and you gave me drink, I was a stranger and you welcomed me, I was naked and you clothed me, I was sick and you visited me, I was in prison and you came to me." Then the righteous will answer him, saying, "Lord, when did we see you hungry and feed you, or thirsty and give you drink? And when did we see you a stranger and welcome you, or naked and clothe you? And when did we see you sick or in prison and visit you?" And the King will answer them, "Truly, I say to you, as you did it to one of the least of these my brothers, you did it to me." (Matt. 25:31, 34–40)

We're guilty of glamorizing service. The same impulse that makes us into facebraggers and position-jockeys looks for opportunities to serve that are high-profile or highly esteemed. We gravitate toward service that has high visibility, looking for opportunities to serve that elicit compliments. Yet we ignore the simple, boring, everyday opportunities to serve family, friends, and people who can never pay us back. We might fly across the world to feed children in a ghetto but ignore our neighbors who need help carrying in their groceries.

Gospel-motivated service looks only to the approval of the God who calls us to serve. It may never result in recognition in this life, but when we consider the recognition that awaits when Jesus comes into his kingdom, why would we hesitate?

And just as God invites us to serve, he equips us to serve. God made us to be like him, living our lives in service of others, doing "good works" for his glory and the good of those around us. That means we're wired to be serving and building up others. As Peter says: "As each has received a gift, use it to serve one another, as good stewards of God's varied grace" (1 Pet. 4:10).

God wired us up with unique gifts that provide avenues for unique service. Sometimes this gets overly complicated, and we're told we need to "discover our spiritual gifts," a process that requires taking tests and learning a new language (like what the "gift of helps" means). But frankly, it doesn't have to be nearly that complicated. Ask yourself, "What am I good at?" Ask the same question to some people who know you well, and then ask, "How can I serve people with that gift?"

Service is a responsibility we're given. "As each has received a gift . . ." We must recognize that there are no accidental talents. God has made you just the way you are so that you can serve his church and demonstrate selfless love to the world. That's the way we were meant to be when he created us, and it's how he's remaking us in Jesus. As Paul puts it: "For we are his workmanship, created in Christ Jesus for good works, which God prepared beforehand, that we should walk in them" (Eph. 2:10).

What Kind of Servant Are You?

As followers of Jesus, then, we can find ourselves in one of three places:

- I am a self-servant.
- I am a selective servant.
- I am a servant of all.

Being a self-servant is a dissatisfying trap. We weren't made to serve ourselves, and doing so sends us into a spiral of misery. In our desperation, we throw our lives into an effort to prove our worth and glory, but those efforts inevitably disappoint, leaving us more empty than when we started. What's the response? We try again, and our need for glory and worth becomes greater and more painful as we continually fail to fill it. Spend an afternoon on Facebook, and you'll see how dissatisfying it feels.

The next option isn't much different. As selective servants, our willingness to serve others is actually just a façade for more self-service. It comes in the form of glorious Martha-Stewart–inspired dinner parties, or acts of service that take place on a platform or in front of cameras. It's the same spirit that leads presidents to soup kitchens for thirty minutes on national holidays; while there may be some sincerity in there, it's mostly just about the cameras. It's service on my time, my schedule, my location, my priorities. It's the Christian who digs wells twice a year in an impoverished country and wouldn't loan you a lawn mower to save your life. It's hospitality with the implied expectation of payback.

And it's antigospel. Imagine how weakened Jesus's testimony to the disciples would have been if, the moment he finished washing their feet, he kicked up his own and said, "Who's got me? I'm next."

Being a servant of all begins with the transforming power of the gospel. As people who have been given everything we need in Christ, we can look at the world around us with eyes open for the opportunity to share our abundance. There is no opportunity too meager, too demeaning, too private, or too public. Because service isn't about us—it's about those we serve and the God who's given us everything. Nothing was beneath Jesus's dignity in service.

Hear the Invitation

Living out our identity as servants isn't a crushing demand but a gentle invitation: "Blessed are you if you do them" (John 13:17). We can begin in small steps, discovering the light weight and easy yoke of this burden, which we'll discover is so much lighter and easier than the burden of self-glory. An easy way to think about it is to "be where you are." Take advantage of the opportunities that already surround you to live out and experience the blessing of serving.

An easy place to begin is to look at the needs in your church family. Most of them aren't glorious—handing out bulletins, wiping noses, hauling trash, or mowing yards. Many of the tasks are similar to the necessary work that keeps our homes functioning with some measure of civility. They're chores, and they need getting done. This is not to demean them but to point to their simplicity and encourage you to see that even here—trifolding papers on Saturday night or demonstrating the proper way to dance to "Father Abraham"—is a place where the invitation to learn to serve can begin. Imagine a church where gospel-changed hearts mark every act of service, where people who know they're loved can, in their abundance, love you by helping you park your car or usher your kids to class. Such acts will cover the place in an aroma of service, like a home filled with the smell of fresh baked bread.

Another place to look for opportunities to serve is at work. Since being a servant is an identity, not a role we play, we should carry out our work with an eye to lovingly serve those around us. Perhaps that means putting down the laptop or book at a lunch break and taking time to get to know our coworkers. Sometimes the greatest act of service is to simply listen to someone, and that can be burdensome. Sitting through an awkward conversation or enduring an annoying coworker is a chance to suffer for the sake of the gospel.

"Really? Isn't that overstating it a bit? Isn't that title reserved for people who smuggle Bibles and risk getting shot?"

Certainly, some suffering is more dramatic and more challenging, but how can we imagine ourselves ready to face persecution if we can't endure inane coworkers? Being present and compassionate to the people God has placed in our lives (especially the irritating ones) is a very practical way of learning to serve.

And of course, there are our homes and our families. For some of us, home is a chaos of diapers and tears, or a battle of wills with teenagers, or a stormy season with our spouses. What if we entered into our homes determined to be present, to look for ways to show love and comfort to our family? Paul says, "Love one another with brotherly affection. Outdo one another in showing honor" (Rom. 12:10). What if that was the mission statement in our homes? What if instead of seeing what our family members can do for us, we start a secret competition in our minds to see if we can outserve them?

Seeking glory in our service is a constant temptation. Until Jesus returns or takes us home, our souls will be perpetually at war with the sin that lives in us. One discipline worth adopting is what the saints before us called "the discipline of secrecy." It's a simple practice: do something to serve others, and don't tell anyone but God. Anonymously mow a friend's lawn. Leave a cash gift for a struggling newlywed couple or parents with a newborn. Anonymously pay the bill of strangers at a restaurant. Get creative about looking for ways to secretly bless those around you. The author of Hebrews urges us to be creative, thoughtful, and intentional in encouraging one another toward such work: "And let us consider how to stir up one another to love and good works" (Heb. 10:24).

As family, we're reminded that our journey through the map of the gospel is never alone. As servants, we learn that our journey isn't for our own benefit, but for the benefit of those we meet along the way.

The goal is to genuinely love others without worrying about our own interests, credit, or glory. But it only works if we do so acknowledging that our service doesn't define us. Instead, our service flows out of the fact that God has already defined us, and we're free to live this better, upside-down way.

Some of us need to be rebuked for not serving at all, for living selfish, self-obsessed lives. Some of us need to be rebuked for signing up for every opportunity to serve because we're looking for that service to affirm and define us. Both types of people need to believe that they're totally loved and accepted by Jesus, because that reality frees one type from self-enslavement and the other from an enslavement to the "shoulds and oughts."

D. A. Carson said:

> The Christian's whole desire at its best and highest is that Jesus Christ be praised. And it's always a wretched bastardization of our goals when we want to win glory for ourselves instead of him. When we arrange flowers in the church or serve as an usher or preach a sermon or visit

the sick or run a youth group or attend a prayer group with the secret desire that we might be praised for our godliness and service, we have corrupted the salvation we enjoy. Its purpose is to reconcile us to God for God must be at the center of our lives. The ground and goal of our existence! Lying at the heart of all sin is the desire to be the center, to be like God, so if we take on Christian service and think of such service as the vehicle that will make us central, we have paganized Christian service, we have domesticated Christian living and set it to servitude in a pagan cause.[10]

The gospel frees us from the search for significance in the things we do. It compels us to a life of love and forgiveness, and invites us to experience the blessing of serving others. It's the way life was meant to be.

Map It

Who Am I?

The gospel makes me a servant, and my service is all about the gospel. I am a servant of God. I have been called, created, and saved to serve.

Where Am I?

I am either a self-servant, working only for my own interests, a selective servant, serving only when it's convenient, or a servant of all, ready to meet needs whenever and wherever they arise.

What Am I to Do?

You don't necessarily need to do more things, but just do what you do differently. Be willing to say, "Lord, I want to be a servant. As opportunities come, help me to follow your promptings." Look for little ways to serve, and take a simple step at home, work, church, or your neighborhood. Bring in a neighbor's trash cans from the curb. Watch kids in the church nursery. Don't be motivated by coercion or the flashy temptation of "new" ways to serve, but by the loving example of Christ.

8

Disciples

One thing is sure: You are somebody's disciple. You learned how to live
from somebody else. There are no exceptions to this rule,
for human beings are just the kind of creatures that have to learn
and keep learning from others how to live.

DALLAS WILLARD

So far we have explored three identities of those whose lives have been
transformed by the gospel: worshipers, family, and servants. Forgive
us if we beat a dead horse, but before we turn our attention to the next
identity (disciple), it's worth repeating this truth: Life in the gospel is
not a path of moral obedience, but an invitation to a better way, given
as a gift of grace. Why, after returning to life from the dead, would
we go back to acting like dead people, rotting away and smelling up
the place?

But we don't wake from the dead with a new set of skills and abilities. This isn't *The Matrix*. No one is going to plug you into a machine
and download ten years of spiritual Kung Fu into your mind, turning
you into an instant spiritual black belt. Your flesh still thinks you're
dead, and it will continually rise up to entice you to act like you're
dead. This is bad news.

The good news is that we have a talented and willing teacher who
can show us what this resurrected life looks like. He's made change
possible through his life, death, and resurrection, and he invites us to
follow him into life with God. It costs us everything, calling us to give
up the lives we once lived, but in doing so, we gain everything: life

the way it was meant to be. *Jesus has made us his disciples, and our discipleship makes us more like Jesus.*

Disciple Defined

In his lifetime, Jesus had a group of disciples who followed him, imitated him, and had their lives shaped and formed by him. It was common in Jesus's day for great teachers, philosophers, or religious leaders to have such followers, who would look to their master-teacher to have their worldview shaped, imitating him in their actions, speech, and teaching. To be a disciple is to enter into a relationship with a teacher that not only shapes your ideas, but shapes the way you live. It's like getting an apprenticeship for all of life.

To be a disciple of Jesus, then, means that we not only learn about Jesus (studying the Bible, learning doctrine, etc.) but that we look to the pattern of his life to learn how we ourselves should live. It means that we will not only be able to answer questions about him, but through the work of his Spirit, we will actually begin to look like him.

The apostle Paul tells us, "For those whom he foreknew he also predestined to be conformed to the image of his Son, in order that he might be the firstborn among many brothers" (Rom. 8:29). God's plan for us involves not only our ultimate salvation, but also our transformation into the image of Jesus. Elsewhere he says, "We all, with unveiled face, beholding the glory of the Lord, are being transformed into the same image from one degree of glory to another" (2 Cor. 3:18).

Philosopher and author Dallas Willard says: "A disciple of Jesus is not necessarily one devoted to doing specifically religious things as that is usually understood. I am learning from Jesus how to lead my life, my whole life, my real life. . . . I need to be able to lead my life as he would lead it if he were I."[1] Pastor John Ortberg said that relationships become toxic when one person begins to believe that the other is never going to change.[2] It's toxic in marriages. It's toxic in parenting. It's toxic between friends. And it's toxic in the church. When we look around on Sundays and see the brokenness that surrounds us, we need to know that there's hope for transformation. And we need to know the way forward.

Missing the Point

Unfortunately, we often confuse the kind of learning Jesus had in mind for us with the kind of learning we experienced in our educations. The word "student" is applied with equal weight to the valedictorian and the slacker asleep in the back of math class. In our churches, oftentimes, it's assumed that all we need to do is show up and stay busy to genuinely learn from Jesus.

Sometimes we confuse the kind of discipleship Jesus calls for (an all-of-life reality) with the kind of learning we had to do to keep grades up. Bible studies, Sunday school classes, and small groups are focused on getting right answers and learning a program rather than adopting a kind of lifestyle. It's an approach not unlike cramming for finals; we want to make sure we've got the answers, regardless of whether we've got their reality integrated into our lives.

The result is top-heavy Christians, people with heads swollen with knowledge and bodies too weak to support them. Like toddlers, they stumble around, often into one another, creating messes that end in tears.

The learning Jesus invites us to is far different from information cramming. It's what Willard calls the "school of eternal living,"[3] and it's a school where the blood of Jesus has paid our tuition, Jesus is our Master Teacher, and the Holy Spirit is our tutor, writing on our hearts to not only help us absorb information, but to absorb the character, strength, and joy of Jesus. It's a school where we learn to be what God made us to be at the dawn of creation, his image bearers, living in harmony with him and one another.

Jesus invites us to this school when he says, "Come to me, all who labor and are heavy laden, and I will give you rest. Take my yoke upon you, and learn from me, for I am gentle and lowly in heart, and you will find rest for your souls. For my yoke is easy, and my burden is light" (Matt. 11:28–30).

The Whole Church

Jesus's Students Learn by Grace

Imagine opening your mail one day to find an invitation to a private golf lesson with Tiger Woods or Rory McIlroy. Or maybe the invitation is for a cooking class with Mario Batali, or a pick-up basketball game with LeBron James. In any field, there's an expert whose skills can help open up that field to us. Such experts can help us see approaches that are hidden, techniques that need developing, and abilities that we didn't know we had.

In Matthew 11, Jesus is inviting us to learn from him about life. It's a mind-boggling idea. Jesus is the Word of God, the one through whom the entire universe was created, the light of men (John 1:1–4). He's got authority over the entire universe, and he's the one who even now is holding it all together (Col. 1:17). He is God in flesh, the maker of everything. And he says, "Hey, that life stuff is wearing you out? Come to me—I'll help. I'll teach you how it's done. I know a way through it that's pretty light lifting."

We would flip out at the opportunity to learn from a master. People pay exorbitant prices to get master classes from top musicians or chefs, they rack up tons of debt to attend Ivy League schools, they compete like sharks to get residencies with doctors who lead their fields, or they spend vacation time at baseball fantasy camps, just wanting a chance to experience what it's like to be among players that are at the top of their game. Here's Jesus, truly the master of everything, offering to be our teacher. God himself is looking at you, struggling and straining to make your life make sense, and in his infinite mercy, is saying, "Come here, y'all. Let me show you how this is done."

Yet we're hesitant, even resistant, to respond and follow. Willard has an insightful critique that explores why:

> In our culture, and among Christians as well, Jesus Christ is automatically disassociated from brilliance or intellectual capacity. Not one in a thousand will spontaneously think of him in conjunction with words such as "well-informed," "brilliant," or "smart."
>
> Far too often he is regarded as hardly conscious. He is taken as a mere icon, a wraith-like semblance of a man living on the margins

of the "real life" where you and I must dwell. He is perhaps fit for the role of sacrificial lamb or alienated social critic, but little more.

But can we seriously imagine that Jesus could be Lord if he were not smart? If he were divine, would he be dumb? Or uninformed? Once you stop to think about it, how could he be what Christians take him to be in other respects and not be the best informed and most intelligent person of all: the smartest person who ever lived, bringing us the best information on the most important subjects.

What lies at the heart of the astonishing disregard of Jesus found in the moment-to-moment existence of multitudes of professing Christians is a simple lack of respect for him. He is not seriously taken to be a person of great ability. But what then can devotion or worship mean, if simple respect is not included in it.

In contrast, the early Christians, who took the power of God's life in Jesus to all quarters of the earth, thought of Jesus as one "in whom are hidden all the treasures of wisdom and knowledge" (Col. 2:3 NASB). They thought of him as master of every domain of life.[4]

If we're to take the Scriptures seriously at all, there isn't any imaginable reason why we should resist this remarkable invitation. To put it in Willard's terms, the smartest, best-informed, and most experienced person in world history is offering to be our teacher. It costs us our whole lives, demanding that we lay aside the wearying burdens we carry and take on a whole new light and easy one.

The invitation is also an indictment. Jesus knows that our lives are empty and dissatisfying, that we are weary and burned-out on trying to carry our burdens. In its place, he invites us to carry his burden—one of rest for the weary, relief, and grace. It's consistent with the gospel for the invitation to come to those who labor and are heavy laden. It's not for the folks who have it all together. It's not for folks who, when asked how life is going, say, "I'm crushing it, I'm living the dream." It comes to the weary, demanding that we acknowledge the dissatisfaction in our hearts. And it promises an easier way.

Jesus's Students Carry a Light Load

Jesus tells us that his "yoke is easy" (Matt. 11:30). A yoke is a collar that is fitted on a pair of oxen to pull heavy equipment or large carts.

First-century Jews used the term as a metaphor for living under the law, an image of devotion to God's word and commands.

Jesus springboards off that image to offer us an alternative. Instead of the burden of obedience (and the looming threat of consequences for our failures), we are offered the easy yoke of Jesus, who has taken care of obedience on our behalf.

Being yoked means sharing a load, and the gospel tells us that Jesus has already done all of the heavy lifting. Instead of being hitched to the unbearable burden of the law (which ends up being a noose), we're hitched to the one who has fulfilled it. He's born its burden and says to us, "Join with me. I'll make it easy."

You might be hearing this and saying, "But isn't Jesus demanding? Doesn't he call us to do all kinds of hard things regarding money, sex, service, and love?"

He does. Absolutely. But we must remember something: God has a way of providing us with a way to do the hard things he requires.

While the Israelites are journeying through the desert, God charges these former slaves to build the tabernacle and to fill it with gold and silver objects. Building campaigns are challenging enough in North America, with middle-class incomes and an abundance of resources. Imagine being a massive roving caravan, traveling through a desert, and being invited to be part of a capital campaign.

What God demands, though, he provides. In Exodus 12:35–36, we see that God, through Moses, had asked the Israelites to plunder the Egyptians on their way out of town. They therefore had the resources when the time came to build the tabernacle, and a slave nation came up with the gold their God demanded. What God demands, he provides.

The same thing is true in the New Testament. What God demands—perfect obedience—he provides in Jesus Christ. Jesus's invitation to "take from me" is an invitation to accept God's provision for us, to receive the gift of Jesus himself. This is why Paul can call Jesus "our righteousness." When God looks at us, he sees his Son. So Jesus represents us to the Father as purified. But not only that, he also fills us with his Spirit and empowers us to live that life of obedience.

What God demands, God provides, and so we're free from the judgment our sins deserve (because God sees Jesus when he looks at us) and we're free from enslavement to sin, because he empowers us to learn from him under the burden of this easy way, this light load. It's a gift offered; it's a gift that meets us right where are but doesn't leave us where we are. Jesus says, "Learn from me," hinting at a glorious hope that awaits us as we follow him.

Jesus's Students Are Transformed to Become Like Him

Following Jesus, living as disciples under the light burden and easy yoke of the gospel, is a transforming journey into the image of Jesus. Paul says, "We all, with unveiled face, beholding the glory of the Lord, are being transformed into the same image from one degree of glory to another. For this comes from the Lord who is the Spirit" (2 Cor. 3:18). We behold the glory of the Lord Jesus and are transformed into his image.

You might object: "Isn't that the same thing as getting rid of sin? Jesus was perfect and sinless, and being like him means being less sinful, right?"

Well . . . no. And yes.

First, no. Jesus's sinlessness isn't the sum total of his attributes. A rock is sinless, but becoming like a rock means something more than becoming sinless. It means taking on the quality of a rock: being hard, unemotional (last I checked, rocks don't have feelings), and unaffected by the weather, amongst a whole lot of other qualities.

Becoming like Jesus means taking on his character, his way of looking at the world, his way of loving and interacting with others. It means cultivating a relationship with God like Jesus's own—one of intimacy, depth, and care. It means living a life that's at war with evil's grip on the world around us, and that certainly includes the sin in our lives, but to make sin management primary in the Christian life misses the point of the gospel. Our sins are paid for, past, present, and future, and in that freedom we can be transformed.

Paul tells us that this kind of transformation "comes from the Lord who is the Spirit" (2 Cor. 3:18), which tells us that any transformation, like our salvation, is a gift of grace. We cannot control it, manipulate it, or manufacture it; we can only seek it from the One who gives it. It happens as the Spirit of God works to transform us. As John Piper describes it, "Beholding is a way of becoming."[5] As we set our gaze on the glory of God, we are transformed by it, becoming more and more glorious ourselves.

So the next question is, "How does the Spirit of God transform us?"

Jesus's disciples desired to be with Jesus to learn from him and become like him. Being with Jesus, seeing his life and work, and witnessing his resurrection, they couldn't help but be changed in the light of the spectacular glory that was revealed. Back to Paul's words: "We all, with unveiled face, beholding the glory of the Lord, are being transformed into the same image from one degree of glory to another" (2 Cor. 3:18). Change happens as we "behold the glory of the Lord." This is the key to everything.

The glory of Jesus is what ignites the power of God's Spirit. God takes endless pleasure in glorifying himself and sharing his glory with his people. This isn't because God is an egomaniac; it's because he knows better than to celebrate any lesser glory than his own. God is shamelessly self-glorifying, and that's a good thing. If God is truly the most glorious, treasured thing in the universe, then it would be the height of selfishness to let his poor blind creation think that anything less than him could satisfy our hungry and desperate souls.

The best way to be a disciple of Jesus is to allow the Spirit of God to open our eyes to the glory of Jesus. As Jesus said, "Whoever has seen me has seen the Father" (John 14:9). He's the truest thing in the universe, the one through whom everything was made and everything holds together. Because of this, it makes sense that knowing him, drawing close to him, would be the key to making sense of the world. And the Spirit of God is eager to shine light on him. J. I. Packer puts it like this:

> The Holy Spirit's distinctive new covenant role, then, is to fulfill what we may call a floodlight ministry in relation to the Lord Jesus

Christ. So far as this role was concerned, the Spirit "was not yet" (John 7:39, literal Greek) while Jesus was on earth; only when the Father had glorified him (see John 17:1, 5) could the Spirit's work of making men aware of Jesus' glory begin.

I remember walking to a church one winter evening to preach on the words "he shall glorify me," seeing the building floodlit as I turned a corner, and realizing that this was exactly the illustration my message needed.

When floodlighting is well done, the floodlights are so placed that you do not see them; you are not in fact supposed to see where the light is coming from; what you are meant to see is just the building on which the floodlights are trained. The intended effect is to make it visible when otherwise it would not be seen for the darkness, and to maximize its dignity by throwing all its details into relief so that you see it properly. This perfectly illustrates the Spirit's new covenant role. He is, so to speak, the hidden floodlight shining on the Savior.

Or think of it this way. It is as if the Spirit stands behind us, throwing light over our shoulder, on Jesus, who stands facing us.

The Spirit's message is never,
"Look at me;
listen to me;
come to me;
get to know me,"
but always
"Look at him, and see his glory;
listen to him, and hear his word;
go to him, and have life;
get to know him, and taste his gift of joy and peace."[6]

The path to growth and transformation as disciples of Jesus is to put ourselves in a place where the floodlights of God's spirit can shine. Change happens in the human heart when we see Jesus as "more beautiful and more believable"[7] than all our addictions to sin and self.

The Accountant and the Slacker

Scripture's vision for discipleship contrasts with the two camps we often see. Instead of understanding change as something that happens as we seek and worship Jesus, we see it as a burden we have to carry and manage alone. That turns us into one of two kinds of people: accountants and slackers.

Accountants believe that following Jesus means ending each day by summing up the accounts: what they did well and where they failed. Hopefully they can end up with a positive total. "Okay," they say, "I read my Bible, gave someone five dollars, and gave my wife a backrub. That's three positives. I was lustful at work and got road rage on the drive home. Two negatives. So I'm in the positive side: a good day."

For the accountant, progress in the Christian life means increasing the margins. Less sin. More good works. Each day, week, and month is assessed in terms of good works versus bad works, treating God as a CEO who is assessing us based on our performance in improving the good-works profit margin of the heavenly corporation.

The other extreme we'll call slacker Christianity. We all know slacker personalities—people who've coasted by most of their lives by giving the bare minimum of attention and energy to what's required of them.

In the church, slackers have the same view of transformation as the accountants, but slackers find the prospects overwhelming and give up. They believe that the gospel is true, but have made no investment in the Christian life. They even have a theological justification for it: if I believe that there's nothing I can do to be saved, I might as well do nothing.

The apostle Paul would shout a resounding, "May it never be!" to both the slacker and the accountant, or as Robert Farrar Capon puts it: "Baby, there just ain't no way! How shall we who are dead to sin live any longer therein?"[8] Both miss the point of the gospel and the invitation from Jesus to follow him.

The accountant has failed to see that the accounting is done with. The totals have been added up, and because of Jesus's righteousness, we're all heirs of a Warren-Buffet–sized profit margin. Resurrected life means seeing beyond the law to a life that's free from all accounting.

The slacker has failed to see that following Jesus is truly a better way, a lighter burden, and a path of real soul-rest. The gospel isn't just a collection of facts that we accept as truth, it's a way of living with God.

Deep down, we all probably have some accountant and slacker in us. On some days we're accountants, feeling good about our little deeds and acts of God-pleasing. On others, we're slackers, throwing up our hands at the futility of following Jesus and hoping that grace is sufficient while we resign ourselves to the spiritual equivalent of wandering around the house in a bathrobe, eating pizza rolls, and napping the day away.

The scandal of grace is that God welcomes accountants and slackers, but it's nonetheless a tragedy for us to miss out on the opportunity before us to live resurrected life now with Jesus. It's an opportunity to learn from the greatest teacher the world has ever known, who not only rules over all of creation, but dwells in our hearts. Apprentices of various trades eventually become full-fledged masters; they eventually are set free to work their trade or skill on their own. That day is coming for us too, when Jesus returns to rule and reign, inviting all of us to rule with him. "Everyone when he is fully trained will be like his teacher," Jesus says (Luke 6:40). What a wonder, then, to know that we can begin to taste that reality now in the school of the light burden and the easy yoke.

When we've put aside our roles as accountants and refused the haggard and lazy life of the slacker, recognizing that God is the One who not only forgives but also transforms, we can begin to talk about spiritual disciplines.

Spiritual Disciplines

Spiritual disciplines are practices that Christians have incorporated for generations to cultivate their inner lives, practices like Bible reading, prayer, fasting, meditation, silence, and solitude. Countless people have written on the disciplines, ranging from those who think that doing the disciplines will let you see through walls and leap over buildings to those who think they're useless but required. There's nothing grandiose about spiritual disciplines, but they're far from a waste of energy. The point of any spiritual discipline is to put our minds, hearts, and bodies in a place where the Spirit can do his work. Through discipline we cultivate the kind of life that shapes us into the kind of people God wants us to become.

This is true of any kind of discipline. A friend once told me a story about playing the piano. She was in the second or third grade at the time, and had grown up an only child with wonderful doting parents. This meant that she really, really believed in herself. When the day came for the class talent show, students gathered in the small elementary school auditorium, and kids took turns singing the national anthem, doing dance routines or magic tricks, and generally demonstrating some skill they had developed. My friend, eyeing the piano on the corner of the stage, thought to herself, "I can play the piano."

She was certain. She felt it her bones. This was a moment when she would unveil this hidden talent to the world. Brimming with confidence, she took to the stage and sat down behind the keys. A deep breath and then . . .

Disaster. She had never had a lesson. She had never touched the instrument before. She was appalled to discover that it took more than conviction or nerve or passion to play the piano. She was a visitor in a strange world where she didn't speak the language, and the gibberish that poured forth from the wood, brass, and copper in front of her filled the room with a cacophony that was only matched by her shame.

To this day, nearly thirty years later, her face still turns red thinking about it.

To become the kind of wonderful piano player my friend thought she was, one has to be devoted to a kind of life that a wonderful piano player lives. It requires the discipline to practice, to study music, and to learn to think musically. Professional athletes devote their whole lifestyle to their sports: what they eat, when they sleep, what they do when they're not training; they consider everything through the lens of how it contributes to their skill and aptitude.

Paul is thinking along the same lines when he says:

Do you not know that in a race all the runners run, but only one receives the prize? So run that you may obtain it. Every athlete exercises self-control in all things. They do it to receive a perishable wreath, but we an imperishable. So I do not run aimlessly; I do not box as one beating the air. But I discipline my body and keep it under control, lest after preaching to others I myself should be disqualified. (1 Cor. 9:24–27)

Our Christian lives should be marked by focused, intentional, and disciplined energy, not a random hodge-podge of sloppily adopted Christian culture. Wearing T-shirts with slogans or buying the right books is not a good plan for real change. It's slackerism. Likewise, accounting for each page read and moment of discipline as though we were earning God's favor is just as great a mistake.

We should be shaping our whole lives like an athlete, cultivating a mind formed by the Scriptures and a life shaped by the gospel, not because we're earning something but because this is truly a better way to live—because we want to be able to see Jesus as more beautiful and more believable.

This takes intentionality and planning. It means spending time reflecting on where we are right now, where we believe the Lord is calling us, and where we want to be, and then it requires mapping out steps to get there. Like farming, practicing spiritual disciplines is collaborative work with the Creator who calls us his *poema*—his beautiful new creation. The farmer plants, fertilizes, and waters. Sometimes he succeeds and sometimes he doesn't. At the end of the day, the real growth is in the hands of the Creator. So it is with spiritual disciplines—we prepare soil, water the crops, and tend to our souls, but it's the grace of God that transforms us into something new.

We have included a list of resources (pp. 217–19) we've found helpful on spiritual disciplines (excluding the folks who think they can make you see around corners).

Finally, a few practical thoughts about the disciplines. Spiritual discipline doesn't have to be fancy. It doesn't require the perfect Bible, the right pen for journaling, or a serene location. In fact, the more you can cultivate an acknowledgment of God's presence amid the ordinary chaos of driving in cars or the noise of children, the more you're doing a service to yourself.

It's wise to give yourself small steps and attainable goals. If you've never read the Bible all the way through, that's a great goal to accomplish over a year or two. Don't try to do it next month. If you want to learn to pray, get a book of guided prayers (Ken Boa's Face to Face books are excellent) and take a faithful step with them.

Richard Foster once said that the most spiritual thing some people can do is take a nap. We are embodied creatures, and if we're falling asleep every time we open the Bible or start a prayer, it's a good cue that we need to start our Renewal Plan with a sleep plan (and an immediate nap).

Related to that physicality, don't be afraid to think in physical terms when you practice disciplines. Read the Bible out loud and pray out loud. It will change the way you receive the words and speak. Pray on your knees sometime—not because you think it will please God, but to remind yourself that you're in front of a king. (Something to consider: throughout the Bible, we're told to assume many postures before God—standing, kneeling, lying prostrate, but never sitting down.) If you always pray with your head bowed, try praying with your eyes heavenward, or with open arms.

Whatever you do, seek to build practices into your everyday life, throughout the day, and keep things simple. Listen to an audio Bible on the way to work. Pray for fifteen minutes in the afternoon. Sing a hymn or two with your family before or after dinner. Take one step at a time, and in these small steps, continually ask God to open your heart and your life to more of him and more of his Word.

The Fruit of Discipleship: Rest

If Jesus is a reliable source (and he is), then we should expect that our seeking to be with him, through his Word and through intentional practices of prayer and discipline, will result in a different kind of life. Jesus describes it as "rest for your souls" (Matt. 11:29).

When Jesus says "rest," we can't help but imagine all of creation breathing a low, deep sigh. Rest appears again and again in the Bible, starting with the creation song in Genesis 1 and 2 and glimpsed again through the apocalyptic veil of John's Revelation. Rest is how God intended the world. While it's true that Adam worked in Eden, he worked in a context of profound rest.

In a passage loaded with wonder, the creation account ends with this statement:

> Thus the heavens and the earth were finished, and all the host of them. And on the seventh day God finished his work that he had done, and he rested on the seventh day from all his work that he had done. So God blessed the seventh day and made it holy, because on it God rested from all his work that he had done in creation. (Gen. 2:1–3)

Rest appears in a world without sin. There is a sense of wholeness and completion, of enjoyment and communion. It's downright utopian.

Of course, all that changes in Genesis 3, when our great-grandparents decide to get creative about God's commands, and sin enters the world. Thorns and thistles appear, and the harmony of creation is destroyed, leaving us to battle and struggle and making rest a strange and foreign concept. We spend our lives working against the storm of a broken creation. We struggle and strain against the sin in our lives, trying to find a path to restoration and searching for a way to feel relieved of guilt and accepted by God.

At the end of time, when God restores the creation to the way it's meant to be, we'll see a radically redeemed world. The curse will be destroyed, and creation will once again rest with its Creator (Rev. 22:3–5). It's a hope that inspired Isaac Watts to proclaim:

> No more let sins and sorrows grow,
> Nor thorns infest the ground;
> He comes to make his blessings flow
> Far as the curse is found.[9]

In our glorious future, the curse is reversed, and the people of God will rest in his presence. Miraculously, it's a rest that begins right now, as we come to Jesus, take on his easy burden, and learn from him how to live in this shattered and broken world.

Coming to Jesus turns our expectations on their heads. We arrive in the presence of God, whose wrath we should fear and whose holiness should terrify us, yet he gives us rest. Not wrath. Not judgment. Not condemnation. Rest. Rest from struggling, proving, earning, laboring, and losing. We're given an easy yoke and a light burden. The membership dues are no greater than the entrance fee—and Jesus has taken care of them both. "Y'all just come on in," he says, again and again. "The laboring is done with, and I'm not starting it up again."

Often we find ourselves feeling like we've started at the bottom again. Our inner accountant seems to think things are going great, we feel like we're growing in character and wisdom and strength, and a moment sneaks up on us and shines a light on how, in spite of our efforts, we remain weak and broken. The illusion we believe in that moment is that we're starting over again, sent back to the starting line without so much as a pat on the head, and we're left as discouraged as ever.

But Jesus's invitation is into a life where that's just not the case. You can cease your worries about starting back at square one because in Christ, you actually began at the finish line. And because Jesus is the one who got you to the finish line, nothing in your power—not even your sin—is going to take you away from that finish line. So you can rest.

Map It

Who Am I?

The gospel makes me a disciple, and my discipleship is all about the gospel. I am a continuing student of Jesus, loved by the Father and empowered by the Spirit, and I creatively seek to live in the good of the gospel.

Where Am I?

I'm either a dropout, "getting by," or a serious student. Dropouts have stopped growing and learning. They've fooled themselves into believing they know all they need to know, and they've grown all they need to grow. Those who are "getting by" want to put in minimal effort, believing they'll squeak by with passing grades.

A serious student of Jesus, on the other hand, knows that the gospel has freed him from earning any grades at all, but nonetheless is a serious disciple for the joy of knowing and learning from Jesus. Serious students learn and grow because they know it's the key to a joy-filled life.

What Am I to Do?

I will work out my salvation as God works in me. God gives me the desire to be with Jesus. He not only gives me the want-to, he gives me the how-to. He gives me the power. We're called to work out what God has worked in. How we learn and apply the curriculum of Christlikeness to our lives will look different for each of us. That doesn't mean we can't learn from one another and encourage one another; it just means we need to be aware of differences. Just because a particular habit or practice of prayers and Bible study works for one person, it might not work for you. And that's okay!

If you're struggling to read Scripture, start small. Create a regular habit of reading and praying through just a few verses. Or simply pray a few verses of a psalm. Give yourself small steps to take, knowing that growth will be most fruitful and most permanent when nurtured slowly, over years and decades.

9

Witnesses

To know the will of God, we need an open Bible and an open map.

WILLIAM CAREY

Several years ago, on what was an otherwise ordinary evening, my wife and I (Mike) sat down for dinner. It was by no means a fancy meal—I'd picked up a couple of burritos from Burritos As Big As Your Head down the street. Our apartment was a nice old place above a restaurant on Bardstown Road in Louisville, a street busy with coffee shops, restaurants, bars, and record stores.

Just as we pulled our creaky chairs up to our creaky dining room table to eat the greasy food in front of us, we heard the screech of tires at the car wash just across the street. This was nothing out of the ordinary. In the warmer months, the car wash was always abuzz with cars blasting hip-hop while little four-cylinder cars stripped of mufflers blasted in and out of the lot. Tire screeching was to us like birdsong is to families in the countryside. It was what came next that frightened us.

Gunshots, especially in an environment like an urban corridor, are an unmistakable sound. If you hear them once, you'll never mistake anything else for them again. Less guttural than a car backfiring, but more powerful and abrupt than a firecracker, they hit the air with a broad, flat percussion that shudders eardrums and sends chills up your spine.

Someone was running, swinging a gun in the air and sending bullets sailing across the lot. The screeching tires came to a halt just in front of him. He jumped in a small, black car and disappeared down a cross street. Instinctively I'd pulled my wife from her chair, getting her away from the window in case a stray bullet flew our way, and we sat breathing heavily for a moment without saying a word. Within a few moments I called the police.

"Someone's been shot," I shouted as they answered the line.

The operator spoke slowly and deliberately, with a distinctly nasal indignation. She was far less concerned than I was about the gunshots. "Did you witness the shooting, sir?"

"Yes, I saw the gunman, he jumped in a small black car and . . ."

"What is your location?" she interrupted. I told her. "Is the victim still breathing?"

"Uh, what victim?" I replied.

"The one that was shot."

"I don't know . . . I can't see them."

"But you saw a person get shot?" she asked, getting more nasal and more irritated.

"No," I admitted. "I saw the shooter as he drove away."

"Oh . . . well, sir," by this time, she was Fran Drescher–nasal. "This is a 'shots fired' call, not a shooting."

In spite of my missing that technicality, the police came. Quite a few, actually, and a young man was found staggering in shock a few blocks away, a series of bullets in his chest and shoulders. He lived, fortunately, but the shooter was never found.

On that extraordinary night, something irreversible happened to Sarah and me. We became witnesses. We observed something strange, out-of-place, and stunning, and we found ourselves in police interviews and in conversations with friends, almost unable to contain our story. We told it again and again; that's what witnesses do. They testify. When we encounter the extraordinary, we can't help but share the experience.

The gospel is an altogether different, but no less extraordinary, experience. For the Christian, it's not only a stunning historical story about Jesus, who was born of a virgin, executed unjustly, and walked away from the grave; it's a personal story. While none of us are physical witnesses to these moments in history, we are witnesses to their impact in our own lives. We've seen the power that grace has to change lives and change trajectories. We've tasted mercy and forgiveness, and we've seen how extraordinary that power is. *The gospel makes us witnesses, and our witness is all about the gospel.*

Jesus purposefully made the disciples witnesses to his life, death, resurrection, and ascension. We can see them embracing their identity as witnesses through their constant proclamation of what they have seen and heard (Luke 1:2; Acts 4:20; 2 Pet. 1:16), fulfilling what the Lord had promised through the prophet Isaiah:

> "You are my witnesses," declares the LORD,
>   "and my servant whom I have chosen,
> that you may know and believe me
>   and understand that I am he.
> Before me no god was formed,
>   nor shall there be any after me.
> I, I am the LORD,
>   and besides me there is no savior.
> I declared and saved and proclaimed,
>   when there was no strange god among you;
>   and you are my witnesses," declares the LORD, "and I am God."
>   (Isa. 43:10–12)

Jesus was training his disciples for the Great Commission long before he issued it to them. He made them witnesses to his grace, equipped with his authority, and called to share his message:

> And he went about among the villages teaching.
>   And he called the twelve and began to send them out two by two, and gave them authority over the unclean spirits. He charged them to take nothing for their journey except a staff—no bread, no bag, no money in their belts—but to wear sandals and not put on two tunics. And he said to them, "Whenever you enter a house, stay there until you depart from there. And if any place will not receive you and they will not listen to you, when you leave, shake off the dust that is on your feet as a testimony against them." So they went out and proclaimed that people should repent. And they cast

out many demons and anointed with oil many who were sick and healed them. (Mark 6:6–13)

The story gives us a window into what it means to be a witness to grace. The journey of these early disciples shows us seven things that characterize what it means to be a witness to the gospel.

Movement

Many religions require a pilgrimage or a quest. You travel to a guru or a center of religious worship, such as a temple or a shrine. Jesus could've adopted a similar model for ministry, one that involved a lot of sitting around, staying in one place and waiting for people to come to him. But he didn't. If you read through the Gospels, you'll see Jesus characterizing himself as being "sent," or "seeking" followers and lost sheep. Jesus went and Jesus sent. In Mark 6:6, we see Jesus's movement—"he went among the villages"—and in verse 7, he calls the disciples to do the same.

It's natural for storytellers to seek out new audiences. Imagine going to a football game and seeing a miraculous last-minute end zone catch. Imagine that a friend who attended with you was always retelling the story to you. And only you. Over and over. It would be odd.

A story that deserves retelling also deserves fresh ears. The good news about Jesus isn't meant to be retold only to those who've heard it (though we should be about that, too). It's a message that's meant to go out to those who need to hear it. It's a story for insiders and outsiders.

Some of us feel terrified or overwhelmed by the prospect of sharing what God has done in our lives. We think we need training on the latest techniques to become a witness for Jesus. When you experience the gospel, though, it inspires you to move out of your circle and into the lives of others. We all instinctively know how to be a witness—think about how naturally you can share with a neighbor a recent business success or a new car purchase, or how proud you are of your daughter for getting into her dream college. The problem, for many of us, is not technique but rather a failure to see the power of the gospel at work in our lives.

When I (Daniel) was a teenager, I was one of the "hard cases." I was selling drugs, partying, and constantly looking for a fight. A few people from the ministry of Young Life saw me and my friends, and they made deliberate choices to meet us literally where we were. They didn't invite us to their events or buildings; they came to where we already were. Because of the patient presence and witness, I came to know and love Jesus. I can remember it like it was yesterday—the overwhelming realization that this was true for me, that God would save me from the sins that were destroying my life. I immediately ran and told my friends that I wasn't selling or doing drugs anymore and that Jesus had saved me from my sin. They all looked at me like I was crazy . . . but within a few minutes, one of my friends was running after me asking me what had happened.

No one had trained me to do druggie ministry. I had yet to take a class on personal evangelism. I had simply been invaded by the grace of God, and I told the people closest to me what had happened. I was dead and made alive and, for me, that was really good news. I couldn't help but testify, because I was now and forever a witness to God's grace.

As theologian Darrell Guder says:

> As witnesses, they must bear witness. They are to make known this experience, this intimate knowledge of God and his saving purposes. But the power of their testimony is not to be sought in the persuasiveness of their report, as might be the case with an effective witness in a court of law. Rather, the Spirit, working in the witness, will enable the hearer to acknowledge the truth and relevance of this testimony, and thus will draw that hearer into the witness' experience to share it and, ultimately, to become a co-witness.[1]

We don't necessarily need training or a new set of skills to be witnesses; we just have to believe that the gospel is truly good news.

Throughout the Gospels, Jesus is continually saying that he must go on to other villages (Mark 1:38; Luke 4:43). Jesus's life is a movement toward people who are lost and broken. The incarnation is a story about God, in infinite power and holiness, moving toward us, enduring the humiliation of becoming human, bound up in a body with hands, feet, and speech, living a common, ordinary life for thirty years. It's a movement from the glorious to the obscure, a journey of seeking us out. That movement continues throughout Jesus's life. He moves toward the unacceptable members of society like tax collectors and prostitutes. He moves toward women who were marginalized in a male-dominated culture. He moves toward blue-collar workers like fishermen. He moves toward outcasts who are sick or disabled.

Religion huddles up. It builds up hedges that define who is in and who is out, and it rigorously defends those boundaries. The gospel moves outward. God moves toward us, and as his witnesses, we move outward too, moving toward people who are marginalized and excluded by the boundaries of religion. The gospel should compel us outside our circles of familiarity, to the marginalized, the "least of these" of our society. In fact, something is terribly wrong with our understanding of the gospel if it is not continually moving outward.

A church that isn't witnessing, that isn't moving outward, doesn't have a problem with technique. It doesn't need a new program. Its problem is first and foremost a gospel problem. Witnessing is a natural response to the experience of God's grace, and its power lies entirely in the gospel. If we're not compelled to share the gospel, we should wrestle with whether we actually believe it.

Jesus's movement wasn't merely geographic. It was also a movement toward the hearts of his hearers. Whether it was the woman at the well in John 4 or the great crowds at the Sermon on the Mount, Jesus knew how to speak to the heart. He never sugarcoated difficult truth, never merely told people what they wanted to hear, but he always engaged them with stories that exploded their imaginations, stretched what they knew, and probed the depths of their hearts.

He wasn't a robotic, emotionless presenter of facts. He moved toward people by moving toward their hearts, understanding their desires, and showing how all they longed for was found in him and his kingdom. Our tendency is to think that this requires a program or a target audience outside the ordinary stream of our lives, but it doesn't. It starts with our being witnesses in the ordinary places where we live and work, and it starts with our simply building friendships and getting to know people.

At Sojourn, we gather large on Sundays and small in community groups and in homes throughout the week. One of our community group coaches went to visit a community group a while back, and found this tendency at work.

It was a newer group at a campus that had recently launched, and the group members were eager to do something big and evangelistic. They wanted to coordinate a fall festival or cookout at the campus, inviting the neighborhood around the church to attend. The coach listened, nodding, and finally interrupted.

"These are all great ideas, but let me ask you something. What's the guy's name in the house next door?"

There was a long and awkward pause. Finally the group leader spoke up. "Uh, I'm not sure."

"How 'bout across the street?" the coach asked.

This time the leader knew a first name, but when pressed further, he didn't know the wife's name, the kids' names, or what the neighbor did for a living. The group had a big vision for reaching the "lost," but they didn't have affection for the people living just next door.

The coach, wisely, identified something all too common for us. We're happy to put together projects and throw big events at our churches. We're much more hesitant to befriend neighbors, share life with them, and be witnesses to grace in our ordinary, everyday interactions.

To be sure, we are not anti-event at Sojourn. We throw several big parties at our campuses every year, and we think inviting people to church on Sundays is a good idea, but these things are only effective outreach tools in the context of relationships—people sharing life with coworkers, neighbors, and friends who don't know Jesus.

As witnesses for Jesus, we don't first and foremost call people to a place or a building. We don't call people to make a pilgrimage to the Jesus-temple or to a stable in Bethlehem. Instead, we seek them out, embracing them as Jesus embraces us. Movement can be geographic, but it's often just as difficult to make relational and intimate movement. Consider how many people surround our daily lives, and how great the boundaries are that have been set up between us. It's a cliché to note that in an age of connectivity, people feel more disconnected than ever . . . but it's true. As witnesses to grace, we have the opportunity to extend hope, life, and redemption to everyone around us, and that means we live as a sent people. Some will be sent to the ends of the earth, but most of us are just sent next door. Bringing baked goods will often help.

Community

When Jesus sends the Twelve, he doesn't let them go solo. He sends them "two by two." The witnesses are expected to go out in community. Elsewhere, he tells them: "By this all people will know that you are my disciples, if you have love for one another" (John 13:35). Community isn't just a requirement; it's actually part of the message. As we live our identities in community with one another, we are testifying to the world what it means to follow Jesus. Pastors Tim Chester and Steve Timmis write that "Jesus came to create a people who would model what it means to live under his rule. It would be a glorious outpost of the kingdom of God: an embassy of heaven. This is where the world can see what it means to be truly human."[2]

When God created heaven and earth, the only thing in creation he deemed "not good" was a man without community. We were meant for relationships, and we worship a God who is himself a community. Our love for one another is a testimony to the world about how the members of the Trinity love and relate to one another. As Jesus says: "As the Father has loved me, so have I loved you. Abide in my love" (John 15:9).

The way we love and nurture, the way we correct and rebuke, the way we gossip and fight and slander: all of it testifies—for good or for ill—to the world about who God is and what he's done. When we enter community selfishly and fail to reconcile differences and build authentic relationships, we give the world a tragically flawed vision of the gospel. When done well, community is a window into the gospel and a window into the life of God.

Another reason we're sent in community is that we're all very different. Paul tells us: "But as it is, God arranged the members in the body, each one of them, as he chose. If all were a single member, where would the body be? As it is, there are many parts, yet one body" (1 Cor. 12:18–20).

God has made each of us different, and each of our lives is a gospel story. We've witnessed the same power; we've just seen it from different angles and perspectives. We're also wired up differently, with varied gifts and strengths. Our stories and skills make us unique, able to serve uniquely and contribute to the whole. On the flip side, because we're all uniquely skilled, there is no one who is able to live out our identity as the church alone. We're all dependent on one another; just as the eye needs the hand, the foot needs the knee.

It's very clear to us at Sojourn that witnessing is a community project. One of our campuses is surrounded by people with significant relational, physical, financial, and spiritual needs. Being witnesses in the midst of all these struggles requires many parts of the body. It requires someone speaking up about the need and calling others to respond and help. It requires people willing to serve in concrete, hands-on ways. Being a witness isn't simply an individual project; it's a community effort.

One of Sojourn's worship leaders lives in one of Louisville's most violent, crime-ridden neighborhoods. He invested a season of life into a relationship with one of his neighbors, who happened to be a drug dealer. One day, the neighbor came banging on his door. The neighbor's dog had been shot by a competing drug dealer, and he needed help. One of Sojourn's community groups helped pay for veterinarian bills and stepped into the life of the neighbor. The men in the group began sharing the gospel with him. Others prayed for him. Members at Sojourn gave financially so this man could stay at a local rehabilitation center for three months.

A few months later, this man stood in front of a Sojourn service and shared his testimony, preparing to be baptized. The congregation wept. There were tears not only because God raised this man from the dead, but also because an entire community of people had taken part as witnesses to grace.

Our witness is a communal witness, a single testimony made by the collective voices of countless witnesses to grace.

Authority

As the witnesses are sent out, they're empowered: "He . . . gave them authority over the unclean spirits" (Mark 6:7). In Luke's account of the story, he says they were given "power and authority over all demons and to cure diseases" (Luke 9:1). The testimony of the witnesses is matched with a power and authority that's not of this world, the ability to represent Jesus not only in testimony but in power.

There's no application process for this. No boot camp or spring training. It's a gift Jesus passes on to the disciples and, by extension, to us.[3] After his death and resurrection, he tells those followers:

> All authority in heaven and on earth has been given to me. Go therefore and make disciples of all nations, baptizing them in the name of the Father and of the Son and of the Holy Spirit, teaching them to observe all that I have commanded you. And behold, I am with you always, to the end of the age. (Matt. 28:18–20)

Have you ever had a friend recommend a restaurant, saying "Tell them I sent you"? Or have you ever had a business connection that got you a foot in the door somewhere with that phrase? This is what Jesus is doing. "I've been put in charge of everything," he says. "Make sure you tell them I sent you."

Paul, in 2 Corinthians 5:20, calls us Jesus's "ambassadors." We represent him as we go, and it should give us profound boldness, fearlessness, and confidence. Ambassadors don't have to accomplish anything on their own. They simply stand in as a representative, knowing that the one they represent is able to follow through on all he says. When we proclaim the gospel, we do so with profound confidence that Jesus is going to do what he says; he'll call people from death to life, he'll show off the glory of the Father, he'll heal and restore all things. His reputation is at stake—not ours, and that should free us from fear about what we testify. More than that, it should lead us to faith in the fact that testimony about him will bear fruit.

Simplicity

Years ago, when we were first planting Sojourn, we had an encounter with an angry shop owner in our neighborhood. When he heard that a church was being planted—and worse than just that, a proselytizing church that believed in archaic ideas like truth, hell, and salvation—he sarcastically dismissed us. "I hope you save lots of souls and make lots of money." Those words stung, but they revealed the fear and cynicism in the minds of many who watch Christianity from the outside: it's all about money. It's all about egomaniacs amassing as many fans and as big a coffer as they can.

Jesus spoke to that fear when he sent out the disciples in Mark 6: "He charged them to take nothing for their journey except a staff—no bread, no bag, no money in their belts—but to wear sandals and not put on two tunics. And he said to them, "Whenever you enter a house, stay there until you depart from there" (vv. 8–10).

In contrast to religious teachers (both then and now) who project images of wealth and prosperity, Jesus told them to travel simply and to embrace those who embraced them first. This requires trust in God's provision—take nothing but the bare essentials (don't roll into town in a Bentley wearing an Armani suit) and stay where you land (don't climb up the social ladder of the city, moving in with whoever has the most elaborate house as the movement grows). Simplicity drives us to depend on God. Witnessing doesn't require big budgets, degrees, or props. These can be good things, but they can often give us a sense of confidence in our plan, in our strategy, or in our tools instead of in God's empowering Spirit. It's a call to contentment, and it's a call to restrain the selfish impulses that emerge when the gospel begins to bear fruit.

That simplicity should shape the way we carry out our witness. It's a simple message, and it can be communicated simply. This doesn't mean that God can't use elaborate presentations to accomplish his purpose, but it certainly means that we should never feel restrained from sharing the gospel because of a lack of resources, be they educational, financial, creative, or physical.

Think about your own life: How did you come to Christ? Did you accept Jesus because you saw sports cars and assault vehicles roll onto a theater stage? Or did you accept Jesus because someone shared a story that revealed the power of God? Was it a well-dressed speaker or a profound and simple message?

The church isn't Target or Facebook, and Jesus isn't a politician or celebrity; we don't need a PR firm to shape the message and give it potency. We can simply and honestly share the story we've witnessed and by which we've been transformed.

Receptivity

It shouldn't be a surprise to know that not everyone will respond affirmatively to the gospel. Jesus warns of this by saying: "And if any place will not receive you and they will not listen to you, when you leave, shake off the dust that is on your feet as a testimony against them" (Mark 6:11). Some will welcome you into their homes, and some will not. There's no prescriptive formula for learning who will respond in advance. We're simply expected to faithfully testify and observe the responses.

In the times and places when that message goes unheard, we are to "shake the dust off our feet." This symbolic gesture places the fates of those who reject us in the hands of God. It's not to condemn them (because that certainly isn't our role) but to recognize that it's up to God to judge or rescue them. So we shake the dust off, leaving that place, that encounter, that rejection behind, and moving on with our task.

God is the one who ultimately calls, convicts, and changes hearts. His work is a profound mystery, sometimes working through multimillion dollar crusades at football stadiums, sometimes working through illiterate street preachers. The power is not in the medium, but in the message and the Spirit who opens the eyes of the blind.

Our job, then, is to look for where he's at work, where hearts are open and responsive, where seeds of the gospel are beginning to sprout. We keep our eyes open for evidence that God is softening a heart, whether it's someone who suddenly texts us a prayer request, starts asking questions, or comments on a thread about Jesus on Facebook. We watch for the quiet, subtle signs of receptivity, as people dip their toes in the water, urged forward by invisible promptings of God's Spirit.

A Call to Respond

The disciples followed Jesus's instructions: "So they went out and proclaimed that people should repent" (Mark 6:12). As we discussed in chapter 1 ("The Gospel of the Kingdom"), repentance is often misunderstood as the grudging, painful turning from something we like (our sin) to something we don't like (obedience). We often think it's the religious equivalent of saying, "Eat your vegetables." In truth, repentance is turning from a lesser good to a greater one. It's saying "stop eating out of the trash and taste this feast the Lord has made for you."

By saying that the disciples were preaching a message of repentance, we say that they were calling people to respond. This isn't merely religious dialog or spiritual show-and-tell. It's a testimony that anticipates someone coming to a deciding point. Are you going to keep eating garbage, or are you going to join the King's feast?

A Demonstration of Power

As Jesus did with his own ministry, the disciples were to display the power of God to transform lives. Mark tells us: "And they cast out many demons and anointed with oil many who were sick and healed them" (Mark 6:13). When the gospel goes out, it results in real change. Darkness flees.

The Whole Church

Some of us are tempted to say, "I don't have any crazy stories. I never healed anyone, and I wasn't a drug lord or a prostitute before I knew Jesus. I was just a selfish, middle-of-the-road person." We hear fantastic stories and dismiss the commonplace encounters with grace that we see in our own lives.

Shame on us! Grace is never commonplace. It is perpetually the exception to the rule, the rare gem in a bag of rocks, the pearl of great price, and the hidden treasure.

Every testimony is a tribute to God's power. Boring middle-class lives that are changed by the gospel are still stories about dry bones that came to life. It's always, always, always a miracle. May the Lord give us eyes to see how truly dead we were in order to appreciate how truly alive we are.

The gospel means freedom from the power of our past, whatever that past may be. We've experienced real change, and we should expect real change in those who hear the gospel proclaimed in our testimonies.

And so we say: "But you will receive power when the Holy Spirit has come upon you, and you will be my witnesses in Jerusalem and in all Judea and Samaria, and to the end of the earth" (Acts 1:8).

You're the light of the world: "You are the light of the world. A city set on a hill cannot be hidden. . . . In the same way, let your light shine before others, so that they may see your good works and give glory to your Father who is in heaven" (Matt. 5:14, 16).

You're witnesses to the gospel, to God's redeeming work, to his invitation to life in his kingdom, to the gift of his radical forgiveness at the cross, and to his unconditional love and acceptance. We're sent from a place of unconditional acceptance and mercy, accompanied by the peace of God: "Jesus said to them again, 'Peace be with you. As the Father has sent me, even so I am sending you'" (John 20:21).

To be a Christian is to be a testifying witness, through your life, your story, and your words, to the grace of God. How is your testimony? Are you presenting it faithfully?

Paul boldly proclaims: "For I am not ashamed of the gospel, for it is the power of God for salvation to everyone who believes" (Rom. 1:16). Paul's boldness is consistent with his testimony. If we truly believe that this is the secret of the universe, the greatest news the world has ever known or heard, and yet we act ashamed of that message, it makes our testimony absurd.

If you're crippled by fear of proclaiming that message, then repent—not in the sense of "eat your vegetables," but rethink your thinking. Ask the Lord to open your eyes to the greatness of this good news and to give you uncompromising boldness because of what God has done.

What do witnesses do? They testify. You've been given the privilege of seeing the gospel at work, and you've experienced its transforming power. You've been made an ambassador of grace, so carry out your mission: testify to what God has done, and experience the joy of witnessing as God works through you to continue to call people from darkness to light.

Map It

Who Am I?

The gospel makes me a witness, and my witness is all about the gospel. I am a witness of God sent by God to proclaim the gospel.

Where Am I?

I am either apathetic, embarrassed, or unashamed. If I am apathetic, I lack any compassion for the lost, and thus I lack motivation to share the gospel. If I am embarrassed, my compassion for the lost is overshadowed by my fear of rejection. If I am unashamed, then the gospel has broken through to give me compassion and boldness. I am a witness for Jesus. I am a light, an ambassador, sent by the King of kings.

What Am I to Do?

Be a blessing. Now that might sound too churchy—"I will be a blessing." But in reality being a blessing is God's promise, fulfilled in your life. God has blessed you to be a blessing. To bless is to give life. It's

The Whole Church

clear from God's Word that God is the source of all life and blessing. And God's purpose all along has been to give life to you through his Son Jesus. His purpose has been to bless you with his Son so that you can be a blessing to others, so that you could give life to others!

Part 3

The Whole World

10

The Whole World

I've got no home, but I've got a destination.

THAD COCKRELL

It's worth repeating that everything, from the tiniest particles that make up matter to the most mind-bogglingly large star in our universe, exists because God said it should, and because he holds it together even now. Our whole world belongs to God.

We worship a God who gets his hands dirty, forming humanity from the dust of creation, becoming human and breathing his first breaths in the filth of a stable, and living an ordinary life as a carpenter. His hands are stained with blood and dust as he climbs Golgotha, and his hands are forever scarred by nails as he dies for you and me. The story of the gospel is a story that takes place within our world, beginning in a garden, journeying through deserts, and showing up in the landscapes and living rooms of our own stories, where we first came to know Jesus and hear what he'd done to bring us back to God.

It's a story that God is telling about a world he made and over which he ultimately rules. Though plagued by the curse of sin, it's a world that Christ inhabited and reclaimed. Theologian and politician Abraham Kuyper said: "There is not a square inch in the whole domain of our existence over which Christ, who is sovereign over all, does not cry: 'Mine!'"[1]

It's within that world that we encounter the gospel and live out gospel-transformed lives. If we think of salvation as a far-off promise, something we'll hopefully "fly away" to one day, we miss out on the beautiful things God is doing right now, redeeming and transforming our ordinary, everyday lives. When we talk about gospel transformation, we're talking about our world: the one where we wake up in the morning, earn our living, raise our kids, and go to bed at night.

Though Jesus has ascended to heaven, he's not finished with getting his hands dirty. Now, though, his intent is to get his hands in the dirt through you and me as we live in the world on his behalf.

The gospel is an announcement that forms a people—the church—and those people live out their new identities in the world around them, pointing people back to the gospel message that changed and saved them. It's a practical dynamic, and one that demands that we ask and pray how to live it out, how to make the connections between the gospel and the world we inhabit. Thankfully, we are not without help.

Jesus's disciples once asked him to teach them how to pray. By now you've probably realized that Jesus almost never answers questions or requests the way people expect, and here too, that's the case. He doesn't simply teach them how to pray; he teaches them how to live:

> Our Father in heaven,
> hallowed be your name.
> Your kingdom come,
> your will be done,
>   on earth as it is in heaven.
> Give us this day our daily bread,
> and forgive us our debts,
>   as we also have forgiven our debtors.
> And lead us not into temptation,
>   but deliver us from evil.

> For if you forgive others their trespasses, your heavenly Father will also forgive you, but if you do not forgive others their trespasses, neither will your Father forgive your trespasses. (Matt. 6:9–15)

The World and the Gospel of God's Grace

Jesus's prayer begins with the recognition that God is "our Father" (Matt. 6:9). We begin thinking and praying about our place in the world by remembering that we're adopted children. We belong to him, not because we've earned it, but because he's made it possible. His prayer is a window into the gospel of God's grace.

This is crucial for us to own, remember, and preach to ourselves. Our lives are so guilt-ridden, so beaten up by the "shoulds": "I should have done this, I should have done that." But when we pray, when we look to God, we say, "Our Father." There's no entrance exam, no assessment of our worthiness. God never stops our prayers to ask, "Wait . . . did you read your Bible today?"

I (Mike) remember a New Year's Eve Party in 2004 where we sat around a fire and shared our New Year's resolutions. It was one of the most guilt-laden conversations I've ever experienced, reflecting guilt and shame about everything from reading better literature to working out to fasting. "Read my Bible and pray more" was like a mantra from person to person, until finally someone pointed out the absurdity of the repetition.

Every resolution to read and pray more was driven by guilt. We all said it because we needed to say it (since we were in a room full of Christians), and just the act of saying it welled up guilt about both our failure to do it and our lack of desire to do it. The impending failure in the coming year loomed over us like a storm cloud.

We hear similar things constantly in member interviews and in pastoral counseling conversations. People are beat up by their own expectations about quiet times, diet, exercise, marriage, parenting, and much more. But grace frees us from the need to perform and earn God's favor (or anyone else's, for that matter). As Robert Capon says, "Don't let the false notion that the cosmic vice squad is on twenty-four-hour duty lead you into the even falser expectation that everyone who breaks the received rules will be hauled in and fined."[2]

Sin's power to condemn us has been destroyed at the cross, and instead, we're given God's blessing and presence. He welcomes us to enjoy him and his world as his children. It means, for starters, that we can breathe easy and enjoy the goodness of God's world, freed from the crushing burdens of our sins.

The Whole World

What if, instead of resolving to read our Bibles and pray more, we resolved to believe that God accepted us as children regardless of how pathetic our religious efforts are? If that makes you uncomfortable, you need to rethink what you believe about grace. The Lord's prayer begins with "Our Father," and it does so because we truly are—and will continue to be—God's children, no matter how meager our efforts may be.

The World and the Gospel of the Cross

Jesus's prayer continues: "hallowed by your name" (Matt. 6:9). If "Our Father" reminds us of grace, then "hallowed" reminds us of the gospel of God's cross. It's a perpetual contrast—the radical acceptance we have and the extraordinary cost paid to provide it. "Hallowed" means holy, and it carries a weight, indicates purity, and exposes our own unworthiness before a holy God.

In the Old Testament, deep within the temple, inside of multiple gates and courts, and finally behind a thick wall of curtains, was the Most Holy Place. It was here that a priest, after going through careful, ritualistic "cleansing," would go on behalf of God's people. Here, God would literally show up, a radiant and holy presence that threatened the very life of the priest who entered. This was where the most important prayers—for the forgiveness of the people's sins—and offerings were set before God.

It's this very curtain that tears as Jesus breathes his last breath on the cross (Matt. 27:51). Because of Jesus, the presence that once threatened our lives is now opened up to us in a radical and scandalous way. The cross cleanses us of our sins, and now the Most Holy Place, the place where we can go to meet with God and enjoy life with him, is literally everywhere.

In the Lord's prayer, Jesus teaches us to call our hallowed God, "Father." His dangerous presence is transformed into a presence of intimacy and comfort; he's our dad. Through the cross, life in God's world becomes life in his "hallowed" presence. Every square inch of it is holy ground.

The World and the Gospel of the Kingdom

The opening lines of Jesus's prayer are like a preamble that sets up everything that follows. The preamble finishes with:

> Your kingdom come, your will be done,
> on earth as it is in heaven.

We're God's children who pray "Our Father" (the gospel of God's grace), who never forget that the righteous died for the unrighteous as we pray "hallowed be your name" (the gospel of God's cross). And in these next words, we pray with eyes open, knowing that this world, right here and now, is a place where God is getting his hands dirty, making this place look like heaven through this strange family called the church (the gospel of the kingdom).

God's plan, ever since he cast his first children from Eden, was to restore what was lost. In the prayer Jesus teaches the disciples, he invites them to join him in that work of restoration. "Pray that earth would look like heaven."

From here, Jesus doesn't turn to abstraction and lofty visions. There are no flashing lights or winged creatures. There is no lengthy catechism. There is only an elegant and simple depiction of the earthy, salty, sweaty, ordinary stuff of every day: bread, relationships, and struggles with temptation. He doesn't call us to ignore the ordinary; he wants to transform the ordinary. He meets us in the midst of ordinary living and tells us, "This is all part of my kingdom, and it's all going to be transformed."

Elsewhere, Jesus prays that we would all be in the world but not of it (John 17:15–16). His vision is for us to maintain our place in this world of his, but not to be overcome by it.

Layovers and Natives

Two temptations haunt us as we attempt to connect the gospel to our ordinary lives. The first we'll call "layover Christianity." Being stuck on a layover means we're wasting time, stuck in the wrong place, eagerly waiting for our flight out of town. We're in Detroit, but we just want to get to Palm Beach.

Christians can find themselves looking at life on earth like a layover. We're here, but we're just biding time until Jesus arrives with a cosmic flight to a better place. No one spends time on their layover thinking about transforming their surroundings or investing in the community. It's just a stop—a bump in the road, an inconvenience on the journey. The "real" thing, the most important business, is all ahead of us. The layover Christian is neither in the world, nor of the world.

In stark contrast is the native. The native settles into life wherever he is and, as a native, is indistinguishable from his surroundings. Natives' lives are entirely focused on their surroundings, with no eye for what's to come. They are both in the world and of the world.

The alternative is the life we want to discuss—being in the world but not of it. The church gathers in the midst of the world, remembering the gospel and remembering that it gives us a new identity. It changes how we live, and by God's grace, it changes the world we inhabit.

It's an invitation from Jesus to be who we are, and to be where we are. We're not told to move off into a compound and build up walls that separate us from the world, or to look at our days with a sense that we're trapped in the mire until he returns. We're also not told to accept everything the way it is, to assimilate into the broken culture around us. Instead, we're told to look at everything and pray, "Make it like heaven, Father."

When someone wakes up one day and realizes that his whole world matters to God, and sees the whole gospel unfold in his whole life, it truly changes everything. His sins are forgiven. The pressure is off. He has a message to share. He's now part of something bigger.

Grace says the pressure's off—we're God's beloved children and we don't have to walk on eggshells, fearing that a misstep will lead to being struck by lightning. The cross says that all space is now sacred space, and the dividing curtain between heaven and earth has been torn down—we have an all-access pass to God's presence here on earth. And so the kingdom advances; as God works through God's people, earth becomes a little bit more like heaven.

Paul says: "And whatever you do, whether in word or deed, do it all in the name of the Lord Jesus, giving thanks to God the Father through him" (Col. 3:17 NIV). In these few words, he summarizes the wonder of life in the gospel. When he says, "whatever you do," he's speaking of life in our world. Everything we do is in Jesus's name and for his glory.

Living in the name of Jesus means two things. First, it means that what we do flows from union with Jesus. Elsewhere in Colossians, Paul tells us that we're transferred from the kingdom of darkness to the kingdom of light (Col. 1:13), and our lives are "hidden with Christ in God" (Col. 3:3). We live under the rule of God in the kingdom of God, meaning that God himself is with us as we live, work, play, parent, and rest.

Second, it means that we do all things as Jesus's representatives. We represent Jesus with our words, work, and relationships. It's an invitation, as Dallas Willard describes it, to "lead my life as he would lead it if he were I."[3]

Paul's vision puts Jesus at the center of our activity in life; no matter what it is, it's done in the name of Jesus. Often, we think of Jesus in terms of priorities. Our lives are imagined as a hierarchy, with the most important stuff at the top, and the rest of life taking its place lower down. Jesus is then one priority amongst many—albeit the most important one. Nonetheless, he's isolated as an aspect of our lives.

Earlier in the letter to the Colossians, Paul calls Jesus "preeminent" (Col. 1:18), and tells us that in him, "all things hold together" (1:17), which means that he's not only the most important; he's the all-encompassing priority. Instead of seeing life as a hierarchy, we need to see it as a hub with Christ at the center—the heart of all of our activity and work.[4] Everything we do is done with Jesus in mind. Everything flows from our union with him and represents him to the eyes of the watching world. All of life is an opportunity to display the splendor of Jesus.

The Whole World

We want to explore the world in which we live in five dimensions: location (where we live), vocation (where we work), recreation (where we rest), restoration (where there's need), and multiplication (where we reproduce).[5]

Location: Where We Live

The first place where we all hunger to see the gospel at work is in our homes. Marriage and family were God's ideas, and his design for them was beautiful and perfect. One can only imagine what it must have been like in the first marriage, to experience friendship, love, and human sexuality without sin. Parenting was intended to occur in an environment without rebellion, without lorded authority, and without abuse or betrayal. Sin's entry to the world introduced discord and strife in our homes, leading to battles over authority and responsibility, and the family has been struggling ever since.

Jesus wants us to pray, "God, let your kingdom come in my home, in my marriage, and in my neighborhood." Such a prayer invites our imaginations into unexplored territory, a place where peace and love rule out over bitterness and where old wounds have the opportunity to heal. But it doesn't stand over us as a mountain to climb. The quality of our marriages is not God's litmus test for separating sheep and goats. Our parenting skills aren't part of some spiritual obstacle course.

Grace abounds for us as we struggle and inevitably fail in our homes, but it also invites us into a new way of being. If we truly have nothing to prove, then there's no reason to put on a show for the world. The model of a "good Christian family" can be an oppressive taskmaster, creating families with neatly mown lawns and tightly tied tennis shoes who are dying on the inside. Such families have all the outward signs of familial bliss—obedience, submission, and good personal hygiene—but on the inside, they are cold, dusty, and full of dead men's bones: "Whitewashed tombs" (Matt. 23:27).

We don't want our children growing up thinking that Christianity is an external thing, a list of rules to obey and people to accommodate. Inevitably, kids who live in that kind of a world discover that it's a hollow existence, and the consequences are painful for everyone.

The alternative is life in the gospel, where we let our kids (and the world around us) see that Mommy and Daddy are sinners in desperate need of the mercy of God. We need our marriages and parenting covered in Jesus's blood, overflowing with his grace and mercy. We need his resurrecting and life-giving power to turn our mess into something beautiful.

The message we need to proclaim to our spouses, kids, parents, and neighbors is, "I need Christ. I need Christ and his death and resurrection to live each day, moment by moment. And so do you."

Be Who You Are, Where You Are

Thankfully, Jesus doesn't leave us where he finds us. His saving grace is motivating grace, and it transforms us from the inside out. The identities we have been exploring—that we are worshipers, family, servants, disciples, and witnesses—are realities that get fleshed out each and every day as we respond to the gospel in the midst of our circumstances.

So because we are worshipers, we can worship anywhere—at home, in our cars, over the dinner table, or in the midst of financial or legal trials. Because serving is who we are (not merely something we do), we stop keeping score. No longer do we think, "I'll take out the trash if you do the dishes," because we've met Jesus, our King, who rules over his subjects and washes their feet. We follow him with a basin and towel, or as Paul said, "Outdo one another in showing honor" (Rom. 12:10).

We take courage as we struggle and grow because we're disciples, looking at Jesus, learning, growing, and repenting. This is the essence of being with Jesus and becoming like Jesus. Typically, when it comes to our homes and families, Christians are overwhelmed. We hear the same things, over and over again:

- I should be waking up earlier and spending time with God.
- I should be reading more Christian books.

- I should be praying with my wife.
- I should be managing my finances better.
- I should be leading my family in devotions.
- I should be witnessing to my neighbors.

It's the same cycle, repeated year after year. We recommit ourselves to a laundry list of "shoulds" and "oughts," and the list crushes us as we inevitably fail to live up to it.

The problem isn't the goals themselves; it's the posture of our hearts. Instead of a pile of burdens, life with God is a series of invitations; we're invited to know him, to immerse ourselves in his Word, and to invest in our families and point them to him. The question isn't, "What's my obligation?"; it's, "What's my invitation? How is God inviting me, right here and now, into life with him, into an experience with him in the midst of my ordinary circumstances?"

The answer may well be on that list above, but the motivation and the ability to pursue it is entirely different if it flows from God, who is transforming us into worshipers, servants, learners, disciples, and witnesses. Instead of thinking, "I should lead my home," we discover that God is inviting and enabling us to do so. Instead of thinking, "I should evangelize my neighbors," we discover that God has made us a witness to his grace. We have a story to tell, and a reason to tell it.

Despair or Deification

When we begin to think practically about what it means for the gospel to transform our homes, we discover two poles toward which Christians are continually pulled. One pole is despair: we're overwhelmed by "shoulds" and "oughts" and unable to courageously move forward. The other pole is the temptation to deify the home: we want to make the whole of the Christian life about the nuclear family and about having a great marriage and raising our children right.

For a young parent, it's a minefield. Word gets out that you have a baby on the way, and you're bombarded by militant, my-way-or-the-highway parents who flood you with literature, guilt, and an exaggerated sense of duty:

"This is how your birthing plan should look."

"You're planning on nursing for two years, aren't you?"

"We had our babies at home, the way God intended."

And of course, the guilt-trip doesn't end when the kids are out of their organic cotton reusable diapers. That's when the God's-way-groupies, home-schooling-homies, and courtship cronies start their work, defining the "Christian" way of parenting down to minutia, leaving a flood of guilt and anxiety in their wake.

Somehow, this seems far removed from the message of the gospel. It's a rigid world of burdensome conformity, weighty rules, and exhaustion. A tomb. It's a stark contrast to the gospel's message of rest, of an end to striving, of completion and acceptance in the arms of God.

Pastors need to regularly deconstruct these lists of legalistic expectations. Sojourn, where we both serve as pastors, is a church in the heart of a progressive, urban, and liberal city, and our particular brand of legalism looks a little different from most evangelicals'. The ideal of motherhood, for instance, has needed regular deconstruction. Moms are often piled-on with the expectation that they'll dress hip, deliver their children with no drugs or epidurals, grind their own wheat, knit their own diapers, think global and shop local, lead Bible studies, and have crazy-monkey sex with their husbands the moment the kids go to bed. Women feel crushed and defeated when they don't live up to these strange ideals, and at times it's been necessary for our pastors to step in and make room for diversity in the church. We've written blog posts and hosted forums talking about parenting, child-birth, and vaccines, and our members' classes always feature a heavy discussion about Christian liberty. Legalism is a chameleon, and it hides in various forms in all of our churches. Only the gospel can free us from its tyranny.

If you haven't heard it anywhere else, friends, then listen closely: No one has the corner on what the Christian marriage and Christian family should look like. There is no monolithic ideal toward which we all inexorably march. God's ideal for your home is as unique as the home's inhabitants, and the gospel means that even if you screw it up—if you homeschool when you should have public schooled or if you nurse your kid for six months when you could have for seven months or if you sometimes just need thirty seconds of quiet on the back porch while the madness of three kids whirs along like the world's noisiest clock inside the house . . . it's okay. The pressure is off. Grace abounds, and God is present in the midst of all your decisions, good and bad, and they're all made acceptable through Jesus, who holds them together, sanctifies them, and offers them to God like a beautiful, fragrant blessing.

When we recognize that we're radically, unconditionally accepted by Jesus, we'll discover that the challenges of marriage and parenting are actually invitations to see something broken be transformed by the power of the gospel.

Vocation: Where We Work

For many of us, trying to make connections between the gospel and our homes is familiar territory. Churches often stress the role of the family and provide a wealth of resources to equip newlyweds, new parents, and struggling homes. But when it comes to where we work—our vocation—the church is often strangely silent.

Vocation means more than just a nine-to-five job. Vocation refers to the work that God has put before you, whether that's as an accountant or a middle school student, a full-time parent or a government official. Work is something God built into the order of the universe.

Before sin entered the world, Adam had a job—to care for the garden and its inhabitants. When he sinned, God not only cursed him, but he cursed the ground he worked with thorns and thistles. As Adam fights to bring order to the ground, the ground will fight back, refusing to be tamed. The thorns and thistles might be literal (in the case of someone who works in agriculture) or figurative (in the case of everyone else). Thorns and thistles might be a demanding boss or a seemingly endless project. It might be the laundry that seems to pile up endlessly or yet another paper to write. When work piles up, overwhelms us, and leaves us defeated, it's the work of the curse, the thorns and thistles that relentlessly grow up in tangles and bunches, reminding us of our weakness.

Even so, work itself is a good thing, something we were wired up to do. It's actually something the Bible tells us is a gift from God, and it's meant to glorify God. Our tendency, though, is to make work about us. We seek credit and advancement, and we leverage every opportunity before us to get ahead, to crush the competition, or to make life easier for us. Who would want to bring their work record before the eyes of God? Who would want their self-centeredness at work put on display before him?

As the gospel takes root in us, it transforms the way we approach our work. Our natural tendencies are confronted and transformed by Jesus, who didn't avoid work but brought it a whole new level of dignity and glory by working as a carpenter. Even as he pursued his work in ministry, his work was marked by a willingness to be a servant, to acknowledge the lowly and hurting around him, and to be distracted from his work for the sake of God's kingdom.

When Paul tells us, "whatever you do," he's including the workplace. What if our work were marked by generosity? What if humility were the primary virtue for engaging our workplace, coworkers, students , teachers, or children? What if we saw work as a place to live out our identities—to be worshipers, family, servants, disciples, and witnesses?

Recreation: Where We Rest

Like work, recreation is something that we see back in the origins of the world. God himself works for six days and rests on the seventh, calling that day sacred and inviting us to join him in a rhythm of work and rest. Sacred rest in the Old Testament was called "sabbath," and was set apart as a day of ceasing from work and for worshiping God.

God has essentially given us batteries that require us to live in rhythms of work and rest. We run out of energy after a period of hours, requiring food and sleep to recharge and continue. Our bodies need rest, and our minds need it too.

The Whole World

It's a rhythm we've fought against ever since sin entered the world. We're tempted either to reject rest and compulsively work, or to reject work and make a god of our rest. One person might be a workaholic, addicted to e-mail and phone calls, never setting work aside for a day off or a vacation, working on a laptop from a beach chair, and giving orders over the phone while in line for rides at an amusement park. Another person might be a restaholic. This person refuses work at all costs, shows up late, leaves early, calls in sick constantly, and spends much of life lying around a filthy apartment playing video games and toying with social media.

At their core, both people have the same issue: they've wrecked their lives by ignoring God's design for work and rest. The first is destroying relationships by refusing to set aside work and be present, and the second is unable to build any meaningful relationships because it might lead to obligations or responsibilities.

It doesn't take a career to become a workaholic. A full-time parent and homemaker can just as easily be a workaholic, perpetually exhausted by cleaning routines, terrorizing her family with rules for cleanliness and upkeep of the home. The same can apply to anyone who refuses to rest.

In Christ, we're invited to experience a truer and deeper kind of rest. The author of Hebrews says: "Whoever has entered God's rest has also rested from his works as God did from his" (Heb. 3:10). It's a promise that harkens back to the Sabbath. In Jesus, we're able to experience the rest that God had in mind from the beginning of the world. It's an invitation to rest from our spiritual struggle—we're totally accepted by God in Christ, and we can rest in him. It's an invitation to rest our bodies, minds, and souls.

John Ortberg said that for many of us, the most spiritual thing we could do might be to take a nap.[6] Resting—ceasing work, even for a few hours—is a small reminder that our work and lives are ultimately out of our hands. God's invitation to rest is an invitation to acknowledge that he's in charge of the world and that he can govern it just fine without our help. When we sleep, the world spins along on its axis, and we wake to find that any number of things could have happened, but God hasn't nodded off once. Rest also acknowledges that our bodies are a gift, and that the Giver has required us to steward them well.

As Tim Keller once put it:

> The purpose of Sabbath is not simply to rejuvenate yourself in order to do more production, nor is it the pursuit of pleasure. The purpose of Sabbath is to enjoy your God, life in general, what you have accomplished in the world through his help, and the freedom you have in the gospel—the freedom from slavery to any material object or human expectation. The Sabbath is a sign of the hope that we have in the world to come.[7]

Beyond restful habits of sleep, any talk of rest also has to look at the way we spend time at play. The gospel gives us the greatest reason imaginable to celebrate and play: our sin has been pardoned. Marva Dawn says: "One thing that seems endemic to those who devote their entire lives to serving God, the Church, and the world is that a high proportion of them do not know how to celebrate."[8]

In the joy and freedom of the gospel, we can celebrate, we can play, and we can enjoy our freedom, whether we're feasting with friends, running along trails, or playing video games. Because the gospel transforms our identity, its impact isn't primarily on *what* we do, but *how* we do it, or rather, *who we are* as we do it. I am, for instance, a servant when I'm resting and playing, not because I'm fretting over where the opportunities to serve are, but because it's who God is making me in Jesus, and I'm motivated to serve when the opportunities arise. Theologian R. Paul Stevens says:

> Recreation, paradoxically, is one of those little "works" we do that don't try to prove anything to God or even ourselves. We have been proven, more accurately approved, by Christ. Therefore we are free to play wholeheartedly. We can really get into it. The gospel frees us to rest because God's achievements are what count in the end. We are free to enjoy recreation not with a heavy heart (wishing we were out doing really "Christian" work) but exuberantly because we have gospel confidence.[9]

The Whole World

Volumes have been written on the benefits and necessity of rest—far more than we could say here. In our hurried and frenetic world, the invitation to rest is an invitation to reject the status quo, to look with an eye to both the past—where Sabbath was established—and the future—where Sabbath is fully restored. In between, we taste something sacred in the midst of our ordinary time, even as the world runs on, ragged and weary.

Restoration: Where There's Need

It's to our ragged and weary world that the gospel then calls us, out of peace, out of rest, out of the transforming power of the gospel, to restoration. Restoration means stepping into the brokenness and need around us, and responding as servants and family to help make things new.

We live in a world full of needy people, and the gospel is a message for needy people. To quote Tim Keller again:

> Before you can give this neighbor-love, you need to receive it. Only if you see that you have been saved graciously by someone who owes you the opposite will you go out into the world looking to help absolutely anyone in need.[10]

The gospel comes to us and tells us that we're profoundly broken and sinful. We're in desperate need, and God, who owes us his wrath and judgment, gives us grace and mercy instead. Because of that, we can look at the brokenness and need in the world around us, the people that our society deems unlovable and marginal, and love them unconditionally. The kingdom of God moves forward, spreading restoration and renewal (Matt. 9:13). It comes to the undeserving and to all who cry out, "God, be merciful to me, a sinner!" (Luke 18:13).

When we start talking about mercy and restoration, we tend to jump straight to conversations about homeless shelters and third-world countries. There's no question that the church can and should respond to those needs, but we should also have eyes for the immediate needs in our family and church. How are we looking to show mercy and foster renewal in our immediate families: our siblings or parents, our rebellious kids and offensive uncles? When a member of our church, Sunday school class, or small group loses a job or faces monstrous medical bills, are we ready to respond generously?

Paul says: "So then, as we have opportunity, let us do good to everyone, and especially to those who are of the household of faith" (Gal. 6:10). We're often eager to do good works that get good press or raise our church's profile in the community, but we are called to be generous "especially" to the members of our church family.

It's not always fun to walk alongside someone battling depression or facing financial struggles, but God calls us to be faithful. Seeing restoration take place shouldn't be like shopping online, where we select from among a host of options to serve. Instead, it should flow from an attentiveness to the need that is directly before us.

I (Daniel) can vividly remember years ago talking to an inner-city pastor about my struggle with knowing how far to go when helping those with long-term need and struggles. I asked him, "How do we know when we've gone far enough?" He responded simply, "Look to the cross and ask yourself, 'Have I gone that far?'"

We step into the need as servants, representing Jesus and serving in his name, and we become witnesses to God's grace as he moves people from darkness to light.

An example comes from one of Sojourn's ministry partners called Scarlet Hope. This story begins with a Sojourn member named Rachelle whose heart was broken over the sex industry in Louisville, with its predatory impact on the lives of young women and families. She decided to be a servant, stepping into clubs in the city, serving meals, and responding to needs in the dancers' lives.

Over the past few years, she's gathered dozens of women who quietly serve the needs of Louisville's strippers and club workers, making meals, helping with children, and sharing the gospel. When girls come to know Jesus and leave the industry, the church steps up to meet their needs and support their transitions. One club worker had been in the business for twenty-three years, had won awards and accolades, and had renamed herself "Victoria" because she wanted to be powerful and victorious. She tells the story herself:

> I named myself Victoria because all throughout my childhood I had been victimized, and I thought this was a way that I could be victorious. I was named showgirl of the year, I had been featured in clubs. But as years went on I always prayed for faith but never got it. I became like so many other girls in the industry, taking pain meds to ease the pain of my past. What was really going on was I was victimizing myself. This went on for years, but God was still working on my heart. On Thursday nights a beam of light would walk into the dark and depressing club, it was the Holy Spirit in a woman named Rachelle. God moved in ways I never knew possible! One day Rachelle invited me to Sojourn, and from the first time I came my life has never been the same. The next week I quit my job. I was scared, but I had faith. I have started working at Scarlet Hope and really learning who I am in the Lord. My life went from dark and depressing, full of addiction, to knowing God. My life is full of joy now and I couldn't be happier![11]

Through the hands and feet of God's people, his kingdom continues to move forward, even into the darkest corners of our cities. And when the light shows up, the darkness flees.

Multiplication: Where We Reproduce

The final dimension of mission to explore is multiplication. The whole biblical story reveals a God who calls us to multiply. When he made the first man and woman, he told them to "be fruitful and multiply" (Gen. 1:28). He promises throughout the Old Testament to multiply his people, starting with Abraham (Gen. 15:5), then Israel (Deut. 1:10; Jer. 23:3). When Jesus finished his earthly ministry, he told his followers, "Go . . . make disciples"—go multiply (see Matt. 28:18–20)—and the disciples did just that, multiplying their numbers as the gospel was proclaimed (Acts 9:31; 12:24). The gospel results in multiplication.

If we zoom way out, we can see multiplication on a grand scale, churches planting churches, movements planting movements. From the earliest days of Sojourn, we've been a part of churches planting churches, partnering with denominations and church planting networks, and ultimately launching our own network in the fall of 2011. This kind of multiplication is crucial to the forward movement of the gospel, but it's not just for vocational ministers and missionaries.

If we zoom in on the small scale, multiplication is, at its core, about relationships. Whether it's a relationship between a Christian and a non-Christian, or a mature Christian and a young Christian, multiplication is about passing on the gospel and the lessons learned on the journey as we follow Christ. John Maxwell has said, "People do what people see."[12] For good or for evil, people follow our lead. In the church, whether you're talking about a small group of twelve people or a megachurch with thousands of people and multiple campuses, "people do what people see." If our leaders are overflowing with gratitude and grace, repenting of their sins, and living out and sharing the gospel in every sphere of their lives, then the church will follow their lead. If they're complaining and miserable, living inward lives and refusing to acknowledge their sin, the church follows that kind of lead, as well.

The point is this: We can only multiply the life we're living out. The life we live is a testimony and invitation to follow us as we follow Christ, and the authenticity and transparency with which we live that life says a lot about the gospel we're declaring.

There was a pivotal moment in the early days of Sojourn that demonstrated this reality. Our church was young. Most of the men in the church were single, had part-time jobs, and had few aspirations for working hard and establishing themselves. At the time, there were only two elders, and both were staff members at the church—Daniel and Les Groce. One day, Les made the decision to step down from the staff and restart his painting company, with which he'd paid his way through seminary. His desire was to step out as a role model for all these young men: to demonstrate what hard work looked like, what provision looked like, and how one could establish a career or a business and still love the local church.

His little company—Honest Painters—became a hub for leaders and men in Sojourn. He did exactly what he had set out to do, training men to work and provide, sharing life day-in and day-out as they painted houses and churches. I (Mike) worked for him for a season, and I saw how Les shared his struggles as a father and husband with the men on his crew, subtly modeling for us how to lead a home with Christ at the center. There was nothing abstract or idealistic about it. Those lessons at Honest Painters still reverberate among the men of Sojourn, many of whom are now leaders and elders in the church.

Les and his wife Alison understood that the answer to the church's challenge—a culture of men who were struggling with a sense of purpose and identity—wasn't a new program or men's ministry. They needed a man with a sense of purpose and identity who was willing to open his life to them. A visit to the Groces' house inevitably led to a meal with their family, and often led to late nights, lingering over conversations. They didn't hide their struggles, but you'd see them repent with one another and with their children. Rarely were you the sole guest, and rarely were the front doors locked. You were always welcome. They were multipliers, sharing the life-changing power of the gospel and taking joy as it bore fruit in the lives of their friends.

The gospel is like a living thing, a message that relentlessly and quietly spreads. As Isaac Watts wrote, it's headed out as "far as the curse is found."[13] Jesus made it clear that the kingdom of God would spread and multiply. Its movement is an assault on the gates of hell itself, and those gates are destined to topple as the kingdom moves forward (Matt. 16:18). It advances and multiplies through both bold proclamation and soft-spoken faithfulness in daily life.

As the church, we live with the expectation that God will continue the advancement of his kingdom in our world. We don't always see the changes with our own eyes, but we trust that faithfulness will bring fruitfulness in time. The Genesis charge to "be fruitful and multiply" (Gen. 1:28) is now worked out through the church as the power of the gospel is declared and demonstrated by his witnesses.

Within the church, we multiply disciples, and outside the church, we multiply worshipers. John Piper says: "Mission is not the ultimate goal of the church. Worship is. Mission exists because worship doesn't."[14] We want to multiply worshipers. We want to see a world full of self-worshipers become a world full of God-worshipers. This was the hunger of the early church as they sent missionaries out to the ends of the earth, and they were utterly confident that their hopes would be answered in a world transformed by the gospel.

Jesus himself foretold this when he said: "And I, when I am lifted up from the earth, will draw all people to myself" (John 12:32). Paul affirmed it too, saying: "At the name of Jesus every knee should bow, in heaven and on earth and under the earth" (Phil. 2:10). And in John's vision of final things, he sees that mission has resulted in worshipers from every tribe and tongue:

> Worthy are you to take the scroll
> and to open its seals,
> for you were slain, and by your blood you ransomed people for God
> from every tribe and language and people and nation. (Rev. 5:9)

Such a vision calls for boldness and fearlessness. This is the end goal of history—a world restored to God, worshiping him once again. Because we know the ending of the story, we can send and be sent, seeking to multiply the gospel in unreached and burned-out corners of the world. That world includes our homes, workplaces, recreational places, and the places that smolder with need.

The gospel has made us worshipers, restoring us to relationship with our God and Maker, and through us, it continues to extend the invitation to the world, saying, "Good news! Life with God is available again through Jesus Christ!"

From beginning to end, we never get far from that message. It's where relationship with God begins. It's at the heart of our transformation, shaping us into image-bearers of Jesus, reflecting back the glory of the very gospel that saved us. And, though we've said it before, it bears repeating: it's where the story ends.

One day soon we'll gather around the throne of the slain Savior, and our eternity will be spent in worship, forever glorying in the God who saves. Even now, we experience a foretaste of that day, as the gospel of God's kingdom—made available through God's cross and by God's grace—takes deeper and deeper root in our hearts, transforming us, and through us, the whole world.

Faithmapping: Journeying Onward

The map lies open on the table. Hopefully you can see how it all fits together. One glorious gospel, in three aspects, forms one church with five identities, who lives out those identities in all the dimensions of their world. The map lies before you not as an obligation, but an invitation to explore. As the old hymn says:

> This is my Father's world. O let me ne'er forget
> That though the wrong seems oft so strong, God is the ruler yet.
> This is my Father's world: the battle is not done;
> Jesus who died shall be satisfied,
> And earth and heav'n be one.
> This is my Father's world: should my heart be ever sad?
> The Lord is King—let the heavens ring. God reigns—let the earth
> be glad.
> This is my Father's world. Now closer to heaven bound,
> For dear to God is the earth Christ trod.
> No place but is holy ground.[15]

Recommended Reading

Whole Gospel General

Darrell L. Bock, *Recovering the Real Lost Gospel: Reclaiming the Gospel as Good News*. Nashville: B&H Academic, 2010.

Greg Gilbert, *What Is the Gospel?* Wheaton, IL: Crossway, 2010.

Timothy Keller, *King's Cross: The Story of the World in the Life of Jesus*. New York: Dutton, 2011.

John Piper, *God Is the Gospel: Meditations on God's Love as the Gift of Himself*. Wheaton, IL: Crossway, 2005.

The Gospel of God's Kingdom

Terry Johnson, *The Parables of Jesus: Entering, Growing, Living, and Finishing in God's Kingdom*. Tain, UK: Christian Focus, 2007.

Martyn Lloyd-Jones, *The Kingdom of God*. Wheaton, IL: Crossway, 2010.

Russell Moore, *The Kingdom of Christ: The New Evangelical Perspective*. Wheaton, IL: Crossway, 2004.

Paul David Tripp, *A Quest for More: Living for Something Bigger Than You*. Greensboro, NC: New Growth Press, 2007.

N. T. Wright, *Simply Jesus: A New Vision of Who He Was, What He Did, and Why He Matters*. New York: HarperCollins, 2011.

The Gospel of God's Cross

Peter Bolt, *The Cross From a Distance: Atonement in Mark's Gospel*. Downers Grove, IL: InterVarsity Press, 2004.

Mark Driscoll and Gerry Breshears, *Death by Love: Letters from the Cross*. Wheaton, IL: Crossway, 2008.

Leon Morris, *The Atonement: Its Meaning and Significance*. Downers Grove, IL: IVP Academic, 1983.

John Stott, *The Cross of Christ*. Downers Grove, IL: InterVarsity Press, 2006.

Derek Tidball, *The Message of the Cross: Wisdom Unsearchable, Love Indestructible*. Downers Grove, IL: IVP Academic, 2001.

The Gospel of God's Grace

Steve Brown, *A Scandalous Freedom: The Radical Nature of the Gospel*. New York: Howard Books, 2004.

Sinclair Ferguson, *By Grace Alone: How the Grace of God Amazes Me*. Sanford, FL: Reformation Trust, 2010.

Scotty Smith, *The Reign of Grace: The Delights and Demands of God's Love*. New York: Howard Books, 2003.

Charles Spurgeon, *Grace: God's Unmerited Favor*. New Kensington, PA: Whitaker House, 1996.

Tullian Tchividjian, *Surprised by Grace: God's Relentless Pursuit of Rebels*. Wheaton, IL: Crossway, 2010.

Whole Church General

Jim Belcher and Richard J. Mouw, *Deep Church: A Third Way beyond Emerging and Traditional*. Downers Grove, IL: InterVarsity Press, 2009.

Kevin DeYoung and Ted Kluck, *Why We Love the Church: In Praise of Institutions and Organized Religion*. Chicago: Moody, 2009.

Tim Chester, *Total Church: A Radical Reshaping around Gospel and Community*. Wheaton, IL: Crossway, 2008.

Mark Driscoll and Gerry Breshears, *Vintage Church: Timeless Truths and Timely Methods*. Wheaton, IL: Crossway, 2008.

Timothy Lane and Paul David Tripp, *Relationships: A Mess Worth Making*. Greensboro, NC: New Growth Press, 2006.

Worshipers

Harold Best, *Unceasing Worship: Biblical Perspectives on Worship and the Arts*. Downers Grove, IL: InterVarsity Press, 2003

Bryan Chapell, *Christ-Centered Worship: Letting the Gospel Shape Our Practice*. Grand Rapids, MI: Baker Academic, 2009.

Clayton Schmit, *Sent and Gathered: A Worship Manual for the Missional Church*. Grand Rapids, MI: Baker Academic, 2009.

John Witvliet, *Worship Seeking Understanding: Windows into Christian Practice*. Grand Rapids, MI: Baker Academic, 2003.

Family

Joshua Harris, *Stop Dating the Church! Fall in Love with the Family of God*. Sisters, OR: Multnomah, 2004.

Joseph Hellerman, *When the Church Was a Family: Recapturing Jesus' Vision for Authentic Christian Community*. Nashville: B&H, 2009.

Russell Moore, *Adopted for Life: The Priority of Adoption for Christian Families and Churches*. Wheaton, IL: Crossway, 2009.

Servants

Michael Card, *A Better Freedom: Finding Life as Slaves of Christ*. Downers Grove, IL: InterVarsity Press, 2009.

John Miller, *The Heart of a Servant Leader: Letters from Jack Miller*. Phillipsburg, NJ: P&R, 2004.

Nate Palmer, *Servanthood as Worship: The Privilege of Life in a Local Church*. Adelphi, MD: Cruciform Press, 2010.

Disciples

J. I. Packer, *Rediscovering Holiness*. Ann Arbor, MI: Vine Books, 1992.

Michael Wilkins, *Following the Master*. Grand Rapids MI: Zondervan, 1992.

Michael Wilkins, *In His Image: Reflecting Christ in Everyday Life*. Colorado Springs: NavPress, 1997.

Witnesses

Mark Dever, *The Gospel and Personal Evangelism*. Wheaton, IL: Crossway, 2007.

Darrell Guder, *Be My Witness: The Church's Mission, Message, and Messengers*. Grand Rapids, MI: Eerdmans, 1985.

John Miller, *Powerful Evangelism for the Powerless*. Phillipsburg, NJ: P&R, 1997.

Rob Plumer, *Paul's Understanding of the Church's Mission: Did the Apostle Paul Expect the Early Christian Communities to Evangelize?* Eugene, OR: Wipf and Stock, 2006.

J. Mack Stiles, *Marks of the Messenger: Knowing, Living and Speaking the Gospel*. Downers Grove, IL: InterVarsity Press, 2010.

Notes

Introduction

1. Karl Barth, *The Word of God and the Word of Man* (Grand Rapids, MI: Zondervan, 1935), 28. Quoted in Carl E. Braaten and Robert W. Jenson, *A Map of Twentieth Century Theology* (Minneapolis: Augsburg, 1995), 23.

2. See the wonderful new book by Jared Wilson, *Gospel Wakefulness* (Wheaton, IL: Crossway, 2011), 24–28, 34–36.

3. Mike Bullmore, "The Functional Centrality of the Gospel in the Life of the Local Church," from Sovereign Grace Ministries' Leadership Conference, 2005, http://www.crosswaypa.org/_files/live/functionalcentrality.pdf.

4. For a helpful overview/primer of John Frame's perspectivalism see John Hughes, *Speaking the Truth in Love: The Theology of John M. Frame* (Phillipsburg, NJ: P&R, 2009), 38–54. Timothy Keller and Edmund Clowney write in their unpublished but widely circulated syllabus, "Preaching Christ in a Postmodern World":

> I think it is important to see that the gospel itself (just like the Triune God) should be understood through three perspectives as well. Each perspective is true in that it eventually comprises the whole, but each approach begins with a particular "door" or aspect.
>
> The "normative" aspect, I'll call "the gospel of Christ", stresses the objective, historic work of Christ that Jesus really came in time-space and history to accomplish salvation for us . . . the "existential" aspect, I'll call "the gospel of sonship", stresses our new identity in Christ as adopted children . . . it will talk much of the power of the spirit to renew broken hearts . . . the "situational" aspect, I'll call "the gospel of the kingdom", stresses the reversal of values in the new creation. It will talk about healed community, cultural transformation, ministries of deed and justice," 82–83.

5. Keller and Clowney, "Preaching Christ," 83.

6. Scotty Smith, *The Reign of Grace: The Delights and Demands of God's Love* (New York: Howard, 2003), 17.

7. Hughes, *Speaking the Truth in Love*, 49.

8. Keller and Clowney, "Preaching Christ," 83.

9. John Ortberg, *The Life You've Always Wanted: Spiritual Disciplines for Ordinary People* (Grand Rapids, MI: Zondervan, 2002), 10.

10. J. R. R. Tolkien, *The Fellowship of the Ring* (New York: Ballantine, 1955), 102.

Chapter 1: The Gospel of the Kingdom

1. Russell Moore, *Don't Call It a Comeback: The Old Faith for a New Day*, ed. Kevin DeYoung (Wheaton, IL: Crossway, 2011), 118.

2. It's Jesus's kingdom language that ends up being used as evidence against him when he stands before Pilate: "Then the whole assembly rose and led him off to Pilate. And they began to accuse him, saying, 'We have found this man subverting our nation. He opposes payment of taxes to Caesar and claims to be Messiah, a king.' So Pilate asked Jesus, 'Are you the king of the Jews?' 'You have said so,' Jesus replied" (Luke 23:1–3).

3. The idea of "good news," for which an older English word is "gospel," had two principal meanings for first-century Jews. First, with roots in Isaiah, it means the news of YHWH's long-awaited victory over evil and rescue of his people. Second, it was used in the Roman world of the accession, or birthday, of the emperor. Since for Jesus and Paul the announcement of God's inbreaking kingdom was both the fulfillment of prophecy and a challenge to the world's present rulers, "gospel" became an important shorthand for both the message of Jesus himself, and the apostolic message *about* him. Paul saw this message as itself the vehicle of God's saving power (Rom. 1:16; 1 Thess. 2:13). See N. T. Wright, *Matthew for Everyone,* vol. 2 (Louisville, KY: Westminster John Knox Press, 2004), 216.

4. N. T. Wright, *Simply Jesus: A New Vision of Who He Was, What He Did, and Why He Matters* (New York: HarperOne, 2011), 69.

5. Dallas Willard, *The Divine Conspiracy: Rediscovering Our Hidden Life in God* (New York: HarperOne, 1998), 21.

6. Richard Lovelace, *Renewal as a Way of Life: A Guidebook for Spiritual Growth* (Eugene, OR: Wipf and Stock, 2002), 41.

7. Some of the most fascinating claims to authority that Jesus makes come in the book of John, where he repeatedly announces his presence with "I am" statements. These are deliberate and inflammatory references to God's introduction to Moses in Exodus 3:14. See John 8:58 and 18:6 (in which Jesus's response to the soldiers is literally "I am").

8. Garrison Keillor, *The Book of Guys* (London: Faber, 1993), 14.

9. See Terry Johnson's *The Parables of Jesus: Entering, Growing, Living, and Finishing in God's Kingdom* (Ross-Shire, UK: Christian Focus, 2007).

Chapter 2: The Gospel of the Cross

1. Tullius Cicero, *Pro Rabirio,* trans. H. Grose Hodge, vol. 198, *Loeb Classical Library,* ed. G. P. Goold (Cambridge, MA: Harvard University Press, 1979), 467.

2. See "The Cross and the Ass Bartholomew" in Michael Goheen and Craig Bartholomew, *The Drama of Scripture: Finding Our Place in the Biblical Story* (Grand Rapids, MI: Baker Academic, 2004), 161. You can see this painting online: "Alexamenos Worships God," *Narrative and Ontology* (blog), Jan. 26, 2010, http://narrativeandontology.blogspot.com/2010/01/alexamenos -worships-god.html.

3. We are using the language of "the cross" as shorthand for the total work of Christ: his perfect life, his death on our behalf, and his resurrection and ascension.

4. See Rob Bell, *Love Wins* (New York: HarperOne, 2011), where he says,

"There's nothing wrong with talking and singing about how the 'Blood will never lose its power' and 'Nothing but the blood will save us.' Those are powerful metaphors. But we don't live any longer in a culture in which people offer animal sacrifices to the gods. . . . People did live that way for thousands of years, and there are pockets of primitive cultures around the world that do continue to understand sin, guilt, and atonement in those ways. But most of us don't. What the first Christians did was look around them and put the Jesus story in language their listeners would understand."

5. Garth Rosell, *The Memoirs of Charles G. Finney* (Grand Rapids, MI: Zondervan, 1989), 58–61.

6. Steve Chalke, *The Lost Message of Jesus* (Grand Rapids, MI: Zondervan, 2003), 182.

7. N. T. Wright, "Putting the Gospels Back Together: How We've All Misread Our Central Story" (lecture, Bristol School of Christian Studies, January 2011), http://www.bsocs.com/page3.htm.

8. Reggie McNeal, Courageous Leadership Conference, Sojourn Community Church, May 12, 2010,

9. Peter Bolt, *The Cross From a Distance: Atonement in Mark's Gospel* (Westmont, IL: InterVarsity Press, 2004), 79.

10. N. T. Wright, *The Challenge of Jesus* (Westmont, IL: InterVarsity Press, 2011), 126.

11. Ewald M. Plass, *What Luther Says* (Saint Louis: Concordia), 1959, 1215.

12. "But I do believe that if you can learn to order coffee at Starbucks, you can learn theological language at church," Ed Stetzer, interview by Trevin Wax, *The Gospel Coalition*, May 30, 2012, http://thegospelcoalition.org/blogs /trevinwax/2012/05/30/connecting-theological-depth-with-missional-passion/.

13. Robert Peterson, *Salvation Accomplished by the Son* (Wheaton, IL: Crossway, 2011), 365.

14. Shai Linne, "Atonement Q&A," *The Atonement*, 2008, Lamp Mode Recordings.

15. Augustus Toplady, "Rock of Ages," 1763.

16. Linne, "Atonement Q&A."

17. Harold Best, *Music Through the Eyes of Faith* (San Francisco: HarperSanFrancisco, 1993), 156.

18. Linne, "Atonement Q&A."

19. John Calvin, letter 22, Calvin to Martyr Salutem DICIT.

Chapter 3: The Gospel of Grace

1. Paul F. M. Zahl, *Grace in Practice: A Theology of Everyday Life* (Grand Rapids, MI: Eerdmans, 2007), 36.

2. "A meal [in the ancient Near East] was never simply a time to ingest food and quench thirst; at meals people displayed kinship and friendship. Meals themselves—the foods served, the manner in which that was done and by whom—carried socially significant, coded communication. The more formal the meal, the more loaded with messages. The messages had to do with honor, social rank in the family and community, belonging and purity, or holiness. . . . Among God's

chosen people, meals became ways of experiencing and enjoying God's presence and provision," Leland Ryken, *Dictionary of Biblical Imagery* (Westmont, IL: InterVarsity Press, 2007), 544.

3. American Psychiatric Association, *Diagnostic and Statistical Manual of Mental Disorders DSM-IV-TR*, 4th ed. (Arlington: American Psychiatric Publishing, 2000).

4. David Brooks, "The Modesty Manifesto," *The New York Times* online, March 10, 2011, http://www.nytimes.com/2011/03/11/opinion/11brooks.html?_r=1&ref=davidbrooks.

5. Jean Twenge and Keith Campbell, *The Narcissism Epidemic: Living in the Age of Entitlement* (New York: Free Press, 2009), 27.

6. Ibid., 246.

7. Ibid., 248.

8. This is a loose adaptation of Robert Farrar Capon's "Creed, Conduct, and Cult" from *The Foolishness of Preaching: Proclaiming the Gospel against the Wisdom of the World* (Grand Rapids, MI: Eerdmans, 1997), 36–47.

9. See Reggie Kidd's *With One Voice: Discovering Christ's Song in Our Worship* (Grand Rapids, MI: Baker, 2005), or even better, the book of Hebrews for more on this topic.

10. Robert Farrar Capon, *Between Noon and Three: Romance, Law, and the Outrage of Grace* (Grand Rapids, MI: Eerdmans, 1997), 284.

11. Martin Luther, *St. Paul's Epistle to the Galatians* (Grand Rapids, MI: Zondervan, 1938), 206.

12. John Newton in *The Voice of the Heart* (Mulberry, IN: Sovereign Grace, 2001), 176.

13. Tullian Tchividjian, *Surprised by Grace: God's Relentless Pursuit of Rebels* (Wheaton, IL: Crossway, 2010), 182.

14. John Newton, "Amazing Grace," 1779.

Chapter 4: Why We Need a Whole Gospel

1. John Frame makes this same point, as John Hughes has pointed out in *Speaking the Truth in Love: The Theology of John M. Frame* (Phillipsburg, NJ: P&R, 2009), 72.

2. Trevin Wax, "Gospel Definitions," *Kingdom People* (blog), June 2011, http://trevinwax.com/wp-content/uploads/2009/09/Gospel-Definitions2.pdf.

3. Craig Bartholomew and Michael W. Goheen, *The Drama of Scripture: Finding Our Place in the Biblical Story* (Grand Rapids, MI: Baker Academic, 2004), 129–30. See Wax, "Gospel Definitions," 7.

4. Richard Sibbes, *The Bruised Reed,* rev. ed. (Edinburgh, UK: Banner of Truth, 1998), 36. See Wax, "Gospel Definitions," 6.

5. John Piper and N. T. Wright, "The Justification Debate: A Primer," *Christianity Today*, June 2009. See Wax, "Gospel Definitions," 16.

6. John Frame, *Salvation Belongs to the Lord: An Introduction to Systematic Theology* (Phillipsburg, NJ: P&R, 2006), 317.

7. Ibid., 324.

8. John Piper, *The Passion of Jesus Christ* (Wheaton, IL: Crossway, 2004), 63. See Wax, "Gospel Definitions," 17.

9. John Piper, "The Gospel in 6 Minutes," *desiringGod*, September 12, 2007, http://www.desiringgod.org/resource-library/articles/the-gospel-in-6-minutes.

10. Fred Sanders, *The Deep Things of God: How the Trinity Changes Everything* (Wheaton, IL: Crossway, 2010), 16.

11. From *Curb Your Enthusiasm*, season 3, episode "Krazee-Eyez Killa," aired November 3, 2002.

Part 2

1. A nod of the head, of course, goes to Rick Warren, Jeff Vanderstelt, and many others who've essentially used these same categories.

Chapter 5: Worshipers

1. Harold Best, *Unceasing Worship: Biblical Perspectives on Worship and the Arts* (Westmont, IL: IVP Books, 2003), 17–18.

2. David Foster Wallace, "David Foster Wallace on Life and Work," WSJ .com, September 19, 2008, http://online.wsj.com/article/SB122178211966454607 .html#printMode.

3. Best, *Unceasing Worship*, 47.

4. This is a time in the service when, traditionally, the congregation welcomes one another with a spirit of peace. Often, it's expressed in a kind of call-and-response: "Peace be with you." "And also with you."

5. Jeremy Begbie, "God's Retiming and Remaking" (lecture, Calvin Symposium on Worship, Grand Rapids, MI, January 29, 2010).

Chapter 6: Family

1. Joseph Hart, "Come Ye Sinners, Poor and Needy," 1759.

2. This was the title of Douglas Coupland's bizarre tale of family dysfunction: *All Families Are Psychotic: A Novel* (New York: Bloomsbury USA, 2002).

3. This is one of many heartbreaking statistics uncovered by United States Department of Justice. For a summary of my studies, see *Angels of Love*, http://www.angelsoflovefoundation.com/Abuse_Statistics_ZJ2D.html.

4. Joseph Hellerman, *When the Church Was a Family: Recapturing Jesus' Vision for Authentic Christian Community* (Nashville: B&H, 2009), 50.

5. Ibid., 50.

6. Ibid., 15–18.

7. Ibid., 50.

8. Russell Moore, *Adopted for Life: The Priority of Adoption for Christian Families and Churches* (Wheaton, IL: Crossway, 2009), 29–30.

9. Ewald M. Plass, *What Luther Said* (St. Louis: Concordia, 2006), 613.

10. Joshua Harris, *Stop Dating the Church! Fall in Love with the Family of God* (Sisters, OR: Multnomah, 2004), 59.

11. Mark Dever, *What Is a Healthy Church?* (Wheaton, IL: Crossway, 2007), 95.

Chapter 7: Servants

1. Tullian Tchividjian, *Unfashionable: Making a Difference in the World by Being Different* (Colorado Springs: Multnomah, 2009), 20.

2. Jean Twenge and Keith Campbell, *The Narcissism Epidemic: Living in the Age of Entitlement* (New York: Free Press, 2009), 117.

3. Andrew Keen, *The Cult of the Amateur* (New York: Doubleday, 2007), 1, quoted in Twenge and Campbell, *Narcissism Epidemic*, 118.

4. Mark Brown, "Cheery Loach and Sneery Von Trier Unveil New Films in Cannes," *theguardian,* http://www.guardian.co.uk/film/2009/may/18/cannes -film-festival-ken-loach-lars-von-trier/.

5. Bob Dylan, "Gotta Serve Somebody," *Slow Train Coming,* Special Rider Music, 1979.

6. Andreas Köstenberger, *John,* Baker Exegetical Commentary on the New Testament (Grand Rapids, MI: Baker Academic, 1996), 400.

7. Michael Card, *A Better Freedom: Finding Life as Slaves of Christ* (Nottingham: IVP Books, 2009), 121.

8. Timothy Lane and Paul David Tripp, *Relationships: A Mess Worth Making* (Greensboro, NC: New Growth Press, 2006), 124.

9. *The Valley of Vision,* ed. Arthur Bennett (Edinburgh, UK: Banner of Truth, 1975), xxiv.

10. D. A. Carson, *A Call to Spiritual Reformation: Priorities from Paul and His Prayers* (Grand Rapids, MI: Baker Academic, 1992), 57–58.

Chapter 8: Disciples

1. Dallas Willard, *The Divine Conspiracy: Rediscovering Our Hidden Life in God* (New York: HarperOne, 1998), 283–84.

2. John Ortberg, *The Life You've Always Wanted: Spiritual Disciplines for Ordinary People* (Grand Rapids, MI: Zondervan, 2002), 20.

3. See chapter 8 of Dallas Willard, *The Divine Conspiracy.*

4. Dallas Willard, *The Great Omission: Rediscovering Jesus's Essential Teachings on Discipleship* (San Francisco: HarperCollins, 2006), 20.

5. John Piper, *The Pleasures of God: Meditations on God's Delight in Being God* (Colorado Springs: Multnomah, 2000), 20.

6. J. I. Packer, *Keep in Step with the Spirit: Finding Fullness in Our Walk with God* (Grand Rapids, MI: Baker, 2005), 57.

7. We're borrowing this phrase from Kevin Twit, Reformed University Fellowship pastor at Bellmont University and founder of Indelible Grace Music.

8. Robert Farrar Capon, *Between Noon and Three: Romance, Law, and the Outrage of Grace* (Grand Rapids, MI: Eerdmans, 1996), 102.

9. Isaac Watts, "Joy to the World," 1719.

Chapter 9: Witnesses

1. Darrell Guder, *Be My Witness: The Church's Mission, Message, and Messengers* (Grand Rapids, MI: Eerdmans, 1985), 42.

2. Tim Chester, *Total Church: A Radical Reshaping around Gospel and Community* (Wheaton, IL: Crossway, 2008), 48.

3. Robert Stein, *Mark*, Baker Exegetical Commentary on the New Testament (Grand Rapids, MI: Baker Academic, 2008), 291.

Chapter 10: The Whole World

1. Abraham Kuyper, inaugural lecture at the Free University of Amsterdam, October 20, 1880, quoted in *Abraham Kuyper: A Centennial Reader*, ed. James D. Bratt (Grand Rapids, MI: Eerdmans, 1998), 488.

2. Robert Capon, *Between Noon and Three: Romance, Law, and the Outrage of Grace* (Grand Rapids, MI: Eerdmans, 1996), 41.

3. Dallas Willard, *The Divine Conspiracy: Rediscovering Our Hidden Life In God* (New York: HarperOne, 1998), 284.

4. This concept is adapted from Ken Boa, *Conformed to His Image: Biblical and Practical Approaches to Spiritual Formation* (Grand Rapids, MI: Zondervan, 2001), 222.

5. We are indebted to Joseph Turner, pastor of Sojourn Houston, for this classification.

6. John Ortberg, *The Life You've Always Wanted: Spiritual Disciplines for Ordinary People* (Grand Rapids, MI: Zondervan, 2002), 50.

7. Tim Keller, "Wisdom and Sabbath Rest," *Redeemer City to City,* http://redeemercitytocity.com/resources/library.jsp?Library_item_param=594.

8. Marva Dawn, *The Sense of the Call: A Sabbath Way of Life for Those Who Serve God, the Church, and the World* (Grand Rapids, MI: Eerdmans, 2006), 56.

9. R. Paul Stevens, *The Complete Book of Everyday Christianity: An A-to-Z Guide to Following Christ in Every Aspect of Life*, ed. Robert Banks and R. Paul Stevens (Downers Grove, IL: IVP, 1997), 853.

10. Tim Keller, *Generous Justice: How God's Grace Makes Us Just* (New York: Dutton Adult, 2010), 77.

11. From a baptism testimony at Sojourn Church.

12. John C. Maxwell, "People Do What People See," *Bloomberg Businessweek*, November 19, 2007, http://www.businessweek.com/stories/2007-11-19/people-do-what-people-seebusinessweek-business-news-stock-market-and-financial-advice/.

13. Isaac Watts, "Joy to the World," 1719.

14. John Piper, *Let the Nations Be Glad! The Supremacy of God in Missions* (Grand Rapids, MI: Baker Academic, 2010), 35.

15. Maltbie D. Babcock, "This Is My Father's World," 1901.

Scripture Index

WHAT IS WORSHIP?

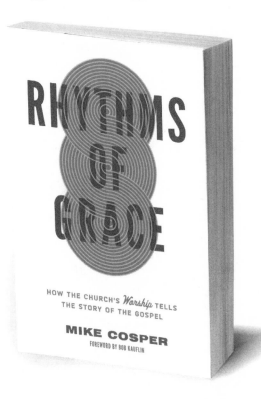

Confusion abounds over how to define the term "worship." Is it singing? A service? Something that encompasses all of life?

Bringing biblical truth to bear on this critical issue, Mike Cosper, an experienced worship leader, helps Christians think more theologically about the nature of true biblical worship, demonstrating how the gospel is all about worship and worship is all about the gospel.

:: CROSSWAY